UNDERSTANDING GLOBAL TREND MARKETING STRATEGY:
USING AI TO FIND THE CURRENT MARKETING TREND

BY
HENRY E. PARKINS

1

COPYRIGHT PAGE

Right reserved, no part of the

Publication may be republished

In any form or by any means,

Including photo copy, scanning

Or otherwise without prior written

Permission to the copyright

Holder Copyright @2024

HENRY E. PARKINS

TABLE OF CONTENTS

INTRODUCTION

In the dynamic landscape of contemporary business, the ability to identify, understand, and capitalize on global marketing trends is paramount to success. The world of marketing is in constant flux, driven by evolving consumer behaviors, technological advancements, cultural shifts, and economic factors. In this ever-changing environment, businesses must adapt swiftly and strategically to stay relevant and competitive.

Welcome to "Understanding Global Trend Marketing Strategy: Using AI in Finding the Current Marketing Trend." This book serves as a comprehensive guide to navigating the intricacies of global trend marketing, with a particular focus on leveraging artificial intelligence (AI) to uncover and harness the power of current marketing trends.

The concept of global trend marketing encapsulates the dynamic process of identifying, analyzing, and responding to prevailing trends that influence consumer preferences, market demand, and industry dynamics on a global scale. It goes beyond traditional marketing approaches by emphasizing the importance of staying attuned to broader socio-cultural shifts and emerging patterns in consumer behavior across diverse markets and demographics.

At the heart of global trend marketing lies the indispensable role of technology, particularly AI, in empowering businesses to gain insights, predict market trends, and tailor their marketing strategies accordingly. AI-driven analytics, machine learning algorithms, natural language processing, and data mining techniques have revolutionized the way marketers collect, interpret, and leverage vast amounts of data to understand market dynamics and consumer sentiments in real-time.

In this book, we will explore the foundations of global trend marketing, examining its historical roots, key drivers, and evolving methodologies. We will delve into the transformative impact of AI on the field of marketing, highlighting its capabilities in trend detection, pattern recognition, and predictive analytics.

Furthermore, we will delve into practical strategies and case studies that illustrate how businesses can effectively incorporate

AI-driven insights into their marketing initiatives to capitalize on current trends and gain a competitive edge in the global marketplace. From social media trends to emerging technologies, from sustainability movements to cultural phenomena, we will uncover the myriad dimensions of contemporary marketing trends and explore how AI can help decipher their complexities.

Moreover, we will address the ethical and privacy considerations inherent in AI-driven marketing, emphasizing the importance of responsible data usage, transparency, and fairness in algorithmic decision-making processes.

Definition and Importance of Global Trend Marketing

Global trend marketing encompasses the strategic process of identifying, analyzing, and leveraging prevailing trends that shape consumer behavior, market dynamics, and industry landscapes on a global scale. It involves a holistic approach to understanding the interconnectedness of markets, cultures, and consumer preferences worldwide, and proactively adapting marketing strategies to capitalize on emerging opportunities and navigate evolving challenges.

At its core, global trend marketing transcends geographical boundaries and cultural barriers, recognizing that trends often transcend individual markets and resonate with diverse audiences across the globe. Whether it's a social movement gaining momentum on one continent, a technological innovation disrupting industries worldwide, or a cultural phenomenon captivating audiences across cultures, global trend marketing seeks to uncover these patterns, interpret their implications, and strategically align marketing efforts to resonate with target audiences on a global scale.

Importance of Global Trend Marketing

The importance of global trend marketing cannot be overstated in today's hyper-connected, rapidly evolving business landscape. Several key factors underscore its significance:

Competitive Advantage: In an increasingly competitive marketplace, staying ahead of the curve is essential for businesses to differentiate themselves and capture market share. By identifying and capitalizing on emerging trends, companies can position themselves as innovators and thought leaders in their respective industries, gaining a competitive advantage over rivals who may lag behind in trend awareness and adaptation.

Consumer Relevance: Consumer preferences and behaviors are in a constant state of flux, driven by evolving societal norms, technological advancements, and cultural shifts. Global trend marketing enables businesses to stay attuned to these changes, ensuring that their products, services, and marketing messages remain relevant and resonate with target audiences across diverse markets and demographics.

Market Responsiveness: Markets are dynamic and unpredictable, shaped by a myriad of internal and external factors ranging from economic conditions to geopolitical events. By embracing a global trend marketing mindset, businesses can become more agile and responsive to changing market dynamics, proactively

adjusting their strategies and tactics to capitalize on emerging opportunities and mitigate potential risks.

Innovation Catalyst: Trends often serve as catalysts for innovation, sparking new ideas, products, and business models that address evolving consumer needs and market demands. By embracing global trend marketing principles, organizations can foster a culture of innovation and experimentation, leveraging insights gleaned from market trends to drive product development, marketing campaigns, and strategic initiatives.

Long-Term Sustainability: Sustainable business success requires a deep understanding of market dynamics, consumer behavior, and industry trends. By adopting a global trend marketing approach, businesses can position themselves for long-term sustainability and growth, anticipating future trends, adapting to changing market conditions, and remaining resilient in the face of uncertainty.

Evolution of Marketing Trends in the Global Context

The landscape of marketing trends has undergone a profound evolution in the context of globalization, technological advancements, and shifting consumer behaviors. Understanding the trajectory of these trends provides valuable insights into the dynamic nature of global marketing and the forces shaping its evolution.

Early Marketing Paradigms: In the early days of marketing, the focus was primarily on product-centric approaches, where businesses emphasized mass production and mass marketing strategies to reach broad consumer audiences. This era was characterized by limited communication channels and relatively homogenous consumer preferences within regional markets.

Emergence of Market Segmentation: As markets became more saturated and competition intensified, marketers began to recognize the importance of segmenting audiences based on demographics, psychographics, and behavioral attributes. This led to the development of more targeted marketing strategies aimed at addressing the unique needs and preferences of specific consumer segments.

Rise of Globalization: The advent of globalization transformed the marketing landscape by breaking down geographical barriers and opening up new opportunities for businesses to expand their reach beyond domestic markets. Companies began to explore international markets, adapting their marketing strategies to accommodate diverse cultural norms, languages, and consumer behaviors.

Technological Revolution: The proliferation of digital technologies, particularly the internet and social media, revolutionized the way businesses engage with consumers and communicate their marketing messages. Digital marketing channels offered unprecedented levels of reach, targeting, and measurability, enabling brands to connect with global audiences in real-time and on a personalized level.

Shift Towards Customer-Centricity: In recent years, there has been a notable shift towards customer-centric marketing approaches, driven by empowered consumers who demand personalized experiences, authentic brand interactions, and value-driven relationships. Brands are increasingly focusing on building meaningful connections with customers based on trust, transparency, and shared values.

Rise of Data-Driven Marketing: The proliferation of data analytics tools and technologies has empowered marketers to harness the power of data in understanding consumer behavior, predicting market trends, and optimizing marketing campaigns. Data-driven insights enable marketers to make informed decisions, identify emerging trends, and tailor their strategies to meet the evolving needs and preferences of consumers.

Embrace of Purpose-Driven Marketing: In response to growing social and environmental concerns, many brands are embracing purpose-driven marketing initiatives aimed at making a positive impact on society and the planet. Consumers are increasingly gravitating towards brands that align with their values and contribute to causes they care about, driving a shift towards more socially responsible and sustainable marketing practices.

Integration of AI and Machine Learning:

The integration of artificial intelligence (AI) and machine learning technologies is revolutionizing the field of marketing, enabling businesses to automate processes, personalize customer experiences, and derive actionable insights from vast amounts of data. AI-powered tools and algorithms are transforming how marketers identify trends, analyze consumer behavior, and optimize marketing campaigns in real-time.

Significance of AI in Identifying and Capitalizing on Trends

Artificial Intelligence (AI) has emerged as a game-changing technology in the field of marketing, offering unprecedented capabilities for identifying, analyzing, and capitalizing on trends in the global marketplace. Its significance in trend marketing lies in its ability to process vast amounts of data, uncover hidden patterns, and generate actionable insights that empower marketers to make informed decisions and stay ahead of the curve. The following points highlight the profound significance of AI in trend marketing:

Data Processing and Analysis: In today's data-driven world, marketers are inundated with massive volumes of data from diverse sources such as social media, web analytics, customer transactions, and market research. AI-powered algorithms excel at processing and analyzing this data at scale, uncovering meaningful patterns, correlations, and trends that may elude human analysts.

Real-Time Insights: One of the key advantages of AI in trend marketing is its ability to provide real-time insights into emerging trends and consumer behaviors. By continuously monitoring social media conversations, online search trends, and other digital signals, AI algorithms can detect shifts in consumer sentiment, identify trending topics, and alert

marketers to timely opportunities or potential threats.

Predictive Analytics: AI enables predictive analytics capabilities that empower marketers to forecast future trends and anticipate consumer preferences with a high degree of accuracy. By leveraging historical data and machine learning algorithms, AI models can identify predictive indicators and extrapolate trends to inform strategic decision-making and resource allocation.

Personalization and Targeting: AI-driven personalization is revolutionizing how marketers engage with consumers by delivering tailored messages, product recommendations, and experiences based on individual preferences, behaviors, and past interactions. By analyzing vast datasets and learning from user interactions in real-time, AI algorithms can segment audiences more effectively and deliver hyper-targeted content that resonates with specific demographic segments or consumer personas.

Content Creation and Curation: AI-powered content generation tools are

enabling marketers to create, curate, and distribute engaging content at scale, reducing the time and resources required for manual content creation processes. Natural language processing (NLP) algorithms can analyze trends in online content, identify relevant topics and keywords, and generate compelling copy that resonates with target audiences.

Competitive Intelligence: AI-driven competitive intelligence tools empower marketers to gain deeper insights into competitor strategies, market dynamics, and industry trends. By monitoring competitor activities, analyzing market trends, and identifying whitespace opportunities, AI algorithms can help businesses stay ahead of competitors and capitalize on emerging trends before they become mainstream.

Optimized Marketing Campaigns: AI-powered marketing automation platforms enable marketers to optimize campaign performance by automating repetitive tasks, refining targeting parameters, and optimizing ad spend based on real-time performance

data. By leveraging predictive analytics and A/B testing capabilities, AI algorithms can continuously refine marketing campaigns to maximize ROI and drive business outcomes.

CHAPTER 1

FOUNDATIONS OF MARKETING TRENDS

Understanding the foundations of marketing trends is essential for navigating the ever-changing landscape of global consumer behavior, market dynamics, and industry trends. By delving into the core principles that underpin marketing trends, marketers can gain valuable insights into the factors driving consumer preferences, shaping market demand, and influencing purchasing decisions. The following foundational elements form the bedrock of marketing trends:

Consumer Behavior and Psychology:

At the heart of marketing trends lies the study of consumer behavior and psychology. Understanding why consumers make certain purchasing decisions, what motivates them, and how they perceive brands and products is fundamental to identifying and predicting trends. Marketers leverage insights from behavioral economics, cognitive psychology, and sociology to analyze consumer attitudes, preferences, and purchasing patterns.

Market Research and Data Analysis:

Market research serves as a cornerstone of marketing trends, providing valuable insights into market dynamics, competitor strategies, and consumer trends. Through surveys, focus groups, interviews, and data analysis, marketers gather quantitative and qualitative data to identify emerging trends, assess market demand, and validate hypotheses. Data-driven decision-making enables marketers to anticipate shifts in consumer preferences, evaluate market opportunities, and tailor marketing strategies accordingly.

Cultural and Societal Influences:

Cultural and societal factors play a significant role in shaping marketing trends, as consumer preferences are often influenced by broader cultural trends, social norms, and cultural values. Marketers must be attuned to cultural nuances, regional differences, and socio-economic factors that impact consumer behavior across diverse markets and demographic segments. By understanding cultural trends, marketers can develop campaigns that resonate with target audiences and foster authentic connections with consumers.

Technological Innovations and Disruptions:

The rapid pace of technological innovation has profoundly influenced marketing trends, transforming how businesses interact with consumers, deliver products and services, and communicate brand messages. From social media platforms and mobile devices to artificial intelligence and augmented reality, technological advancements have created new opportunities for marketers to engage consumers, personalize experiences, and drive brand awareness. Staying abreast of emerging technologies and disruptive trends is essential for marketers seeking to capitalize on new opportunities and stay ahead of competitors.

Economic and Market Forces:

Economic conditions, market dynamics, and industry trends shape the competitive landscape and influence consumer behavior in profound ways. Factors such as inflation, unemployment rates, GDP growth, and industry consolidation can impact consumer spending habits, purchasing power, and brand loyalty. Marketers must monitor economic indicators, track industry trends, and adapt marketing strategies to respond to changing market conditions and consumer preferences.

Innovation and Creativity: Innovation and creativity are catalysts for driving marketing trends, as breakthrough ideas, disruptive technologies, and unconventional strategies have the power to reshape industries and capture consumer attention. Marketers must foster a culture of innovation, experimentation, and risk-taking within their organizations to generate fresh insights, develop innovative products, and create compelling marketing campaigns that resonate with target audiences.

Historical Perspective on Marketing Trends

To comprehend the contemporary landscape of marketing trends, it's essential to explore their historical roots and evolution over time. The journey of marketing trends is intertwined with the broader narrative of human civilization, commerce, and societal evolution. The following historical perspective sheds light on the evolution of marketing trends:

Early Trade and Barter: The origins of marketing can be traced back to ancient civilizations where early humans engaged in trade and barter to fulfill their needs and desires. In this primitive form of exchange, individuals traded goods and services based on mutual necessity, laying the groundwork for future commercial transactions and market dynamics.

Rise of Mercantilism: During the Middle Ages and the Renaissance period, the rise of mercantilism fueled the growth of trade networks, markets, and commercial enterprises. Merchants sought to expand their reach, establish trade routes, and capitalize on emerging consumer markets, laying the foundation for modern marketing practices.

Industrial Revolution and Mass Production: The Industrial Revolution of the 18th and 19th centuries ushered in a new era of mass production, urbanization, and consumerism. Innovations in manufacturing, transportation, and communication enabled businesses to produce goods at scale and reach larger audiences through mass marketing strategies.

Emergence of Branding and Advertising: The late 19th and early 20th centuries witnessed the emergence of branding and advertising as essential components of marketing strategy. Companies began to differentiate their products through branding, logos, and slogans, while advertising campaigns leveraged print media, billboards, and radio to reach consumers and create brand awareness.

Golden Age of Advertising: The mid-20th century marked the golden age of advertising, characterized by the proliferation of television commercials, celebrity endorsements, and iconic brand campaigns. Advertising agencies played a central role in shaping consumer perceptions, influencing purchasing decisions, and driving brand loyalty through compelling storytelling and visual imagery.

Segmentation and Targeting: The latter half of the 20th century witnessed a shift towards market segmentation and targeted marketing approaches. Marketers began to recognize the importance of understanding consumer demographics, psychographics, and behavior patterns to tailor marketing messages and product offerings to specific audience segments.

Digital Revolution and Data-driven Marketing: The advent of the internet and digital technologies in the late 20th century revolutionized the marketing landscape, enabling unprecedented levels of data collection, analysis, and personalization. Digital marketing channels such as search engines, social media, and email transformed how businesses engage with consumers, deliver personalized experiences, and measure marketing effectiveness.

Rise of Social Media and Influencer Marketing: The 21st century witnessed the rise of social media

platforms and influencer marketing as powerful drivers of consumer engagement and brand advocacy. Social media networks such as Facebook, Instagram, and Twitter provided brands with new avenues to connect with audiences, cultivate communities, and amplify brand messages through user-generated content and influencer partnerships.

Shift Towards Purpose-driven Marketing:

In recent years, there has been a notable shift towards purpose-driven marketing initiatives that prioritize social responsibility, sustainability, and ethical business practices. Consumers are increasingly gravitating towards brands that align with their values and contribute to causes they care about, driving a new era of conscious consumerism and brand activism.

Integration of AI and Predictive Analytics:

In the digital age, the integration of artificial intelligence (AI) and predictive analytics is reshaping the future of marketing trends. AI-powered algorithms enable marketers to analyze vast amounts of data, predict consumer behavior, and optimize marketing campaigns in real-time, empowering businesses to stay agile, responsive, and competitive in an increasingly dynamic and complex global marketplace.

Key Drivers of Marketing Trends

In the dynamic landscape of global marketing, trends emerge and evolve in response to a myriad of factors that shape consumer behavior, influence market dynamics, and drive industry innovation. By understanding the key drivers behind marketing trends, marketers can gain valuable insights into the forces shaping the marketplace and anticipate shifts in consumer preferences and behaviors. The following drivers serve as catalysts for driving marketing trends:

Consumer Needs and Preferences: At the heart of marketing trends are evolving consumer needs, preferences, and desires. As lifestyles change, technological advancements emerge, and societal norms evolve, consumers seek products, services, and experiences that align with their values, aspirations, and lifestyle choices. Marketers must stay attuned to shifting consumer preferences and adapt their strategies to meet changing demands and expectations.

Technological Advancements:

Rapid advancements in technology have revolutionized how businesses engage with consumers, deliver products and services, and communicate brand messages. From social media platforms and mobile devices to artificial intelligence and virtual reality, technological innovations create new opportunities for marketers to reach and interact with consumers in innovative ways. Marketers who embrace emerging technologies can gain a competitive edge and capitalize on new channels for customer engagement and brand promotion.

Cultural and Societal Shifts:

Cultural and societal trends exert a profound influence on consumer behavior and market dynamics. Changes in demographics, cultural norms, and societal values shape consumer attitudes, preferences, and purchasing decisions. Marketers must recognize and respond to cultural shifts, diversity trends, and changing consumer demographics to develop campaigns that resonate with diverse audiences and foster inclusive brand experiences.

Economic Conditions and Market Forces:

Economic conditions, market trends, and industry dynamics impact consumer spending habits, purchasing power, and brand loyalty. Factors such as inflation, unemployment rates, GDP growth, and industry competition shape the competitive landscape and influence consumer behavior. Marketers must monitor economic indicators, track market trends, and adapt their strategies to respond to changing market conditions and consumer preferences.

Industry Innovation and Disruption:

Innovation drives marketing trends by creating new opportunities for businesses to differentiate themselves, disrupt traditional markets, and capture consumer attention. Disruptive technologies, business models, and market entrants challenge established norms, forcing marketers to innovate and evolve to stay relevant. By embracing innovation and fostering a culture of creativity and experimentation, marketers can drive industry innovation and shape emerging trends.

Environmental and Sustainability Concerns:

Increasingly, consumers are prioritizing environmental sustainability, ethical sourcing, and corporate social responsibility when making purchasing decisions. Brands that demonstrate a commitment to sustainability and social impact can differentiate themselves and build stronger connections with environmentally-conscious consumers. Marketers can capitalize on growing sustainability trends by integrating eco-friendly practices, green initiatives, and purpose-driven messaging into their marketing strategies.

Regulatory and Legal Frameworks:

Regulatory frameworks, industry standards, and legal considerations shape the marketing landscape and influence brand strategies.

Marketers must navigate complex regulations related to data privacy, advertising standards, and consumer protection to ensure compliance and mitigate legal risks. By staying informed about regulatory developments and industry guidelines, marketers can develop ethical and responsible marketing campaigns that adhere to legal requirements and industry best practices.

Understanding Consumer Behavior and Preferences

Consumer behavior and preferences lie at the heart of global trend marketing, shaping the way individuals interact with products, brands, and marketing messages across diverse cultural contexts and market segments. By gaining insights into the motivations, attitudes, and decision-making processes that drive consumer behavior, marketers can develop strategies that resonate with target audiences and capitalize on emerging trends. The following key aspects shed light on understanding consumer behavior and preferences:

Psychological Factors: Consumer behavior is influenced by a myriad of psychological factors, including perceptions, attitudes, beliefs, motivations, and emotions. Marketers leverage principles from psychology, such as Maslow's hierarchy of needs, Freudian theory, and behavioral economics, to understand how consumers make purchasing decisions and respond to marketing stimuli. By appealing to consumers' psychological needs and desires, marketers can create compelling brand experiences that resonate on an emotional level and drive consumer engagement.

Cultural Influences: Cultural norms, values, and traditions play a significant role in shaping consumer behavior and preferences. Different cultures have distinct attitudes towards consumption, family dynamics, social relationships, and individual identity, which influence how individuals perceive and interact with brands and products. Marketers must recognize and respect cultural diversity, adapt their messaging and communication strategies to resonate with local customs and traditions, and avoid cultural stereotypes or misinterpretations that may alienate or offend consumers.

Socioeconomic Factors:

Socioeconomic factors, such as income, education, occupation, and social status, influence consumers' purchasing power, lifestyle choices, and consumption patterns. Individuals from different socioeconomic backgrounds have varying needs, aspirations, and priorities, which impact their spending habits and brand preferences. Marketers must segment their target audiences based on socioeconomic indicators, tailor their marketing messages to address specific consumer segments, and offer products and services that align with their economic circumstances and lifestyle preferences.

Technological Adoption: The rapid adoption of technology has transformed how consumers discover, evaluate, and purchase products and services. Digital technologies, mobile devices, social media platforms, and e-commerce platforms have empowered consumers with unprecedented access to information, peer recommendations, and online reviews,

shaping their purchasing decisions and brand perceptions. Marketers must embrace digital channels, optimize their online presence, and leverage technology-driven insights to engage with tech-savvy consumers and deliver seamless, personalized experiences across multiple touchpoints.

Consumer Journey Mapping:

Understanding the consumer journey—from initial awareness and consideration to purchase and post-purchase engagement—is essential for identifying key touchpoints, pain points, and opportunities for engagement. By mapping the consumer journey and analyzing consumer interactions at each stage, marketers can identify friction points, optimize the user experience, and deliver relevant content and messaging that guides consumers along the path to purchase. Data-driven insights and AI-powered analytics can help marketers track consumer behavior, predict intent, and personalize interactions to enhance the overall customer experience.

Emotional and Experiential Marketing: Emotionally resonant and experiential marketing approaches are effective strategies for connecting with consumers on a deeper level and fostering brand loyalty. By creating memorable experiences, telling authentic stories, and evoking positive emotions, marketers can forge emotional connections with consumers that transcend transactional relationships. Experiential marketing tactics, such as immersive events, interactive campaigns, and personalized experiences, enable brands to engage with consumers in meaningful ways and leave a lasting impression that drives brand advocacy and loyalty.

CHAPTER 2
THE ROLE OF AI IN GLOBAL TREND MARKETING

Artificial Intelligence (AI) has emerged as a transformative force in the field of global trend marketing, revolutionizing the way businesses identify, analyze, and capitalize on emerging trends in the marketplace. From predictive analytics to personalized recommendations, AI-powered technologies offer unparalleled capabilities for uncovering insights, predicting consumer behavior, and driving strategic decision-making. The following aspects illuminate the pivotal role of AI in global trend marketing:

Trend Identification and Analysis: AI algorithms are adept at processing vast amounts of data from diverse sources, including social media, online forums, news articles, and consumer reviews, to identify emerging trends and patterns in real-time. By analyzing textual, visual, and behavioral data, AI can detect shifts in consumer preferences, identify trending topics, and uncover latent trends

that may not be immediately apparent to human analysts.

Predictive Analytics: AI enables predictive analytics models that forecast future trends and anticipate consumer behavior with a high degree of accuracy. By analyzing historical data, identifying patterns, and leveraging machine learning algorithms, AI models can predict market trends, demand fluctuations, and consumer sentiment, enabling marketers to proactively adjust their strategies and capitalize on emerging opportunities.

Consumer Insights and Segmentation: AI-powered analytics tools enable marketers to gain deeper insights into consumer preferences, behaviors, and demographic characteristics. By segmenting audiences based on psychographic profiles, purchase history, and online behavior, AI algorithms can identify micro-segments and tailor marketing messages and offers to specific audience segments, maximizing relevance and engagement.

Personalization and Targeting: AI-driven personalization enables marketers to deliver tailored experiences, product recommendations, and marketing messages to individual consumers based on their preferences, behavior, and past interactions. By leveraging machine learning algorithms and real-time data analysis, AI can deliver hyper-targeted content across multiple channels, driving higher conversion rates, and enhancing customer satisfaction.

Content Creation and Optimization:

AI-powered content generation tools enable marketers to create and optimize content at scale, reducing the time and resources required for manual content creation processes. Natural language processing (NLP) algorithms can analyze trends in online content, identify relevant topics, and generate compelling copy that resonates with target audiences, improving content relevancy and engagement.

Real-Time Decision Making:

AI enables real-time decision-making capabilities that empower marketers to respond rapidly to changing market dynamics and consumer behavior. By monitoring data streams, analyzing trends, and automating decision-making processes, AI algorithms can optimize marketing campaigns, allocate resources, and adjust strategies on the fly, ensuring agility and responsiveness in a fast-paced environment.

Competitive Intelligence: AI-powered competitive intelligence tools enable marketers to gain insights into competitor strategies, market trends, and industry dynamics. By analyzing competitor activities, monitoring market trends, and identifying whitespace opportunities, AI algorithms can help businesses stay ahead of competitors and capitalize on emerging trends before they become mainstream.

Introduction to Artificial Intelligence in Marketing

In recent years, the intersection of artificial intelligence (AI) and marketing has transformed the way businesses engage with consumers, analyze data, and drive strategic decision-making. From predictive analytics to personalized recommendations, AI-powered technologies have become indispensable tools for marketers seeking to understand consumer behavior, identify trends, and capitalize on emerging opportunities in the global marketplace. In this introductory chapter, we explore the transformative role of AI in marketing and its implications for understanding global trend marketing strategies.

The Rise of Artificial Intelligence:

Artificial intelligence, once confined to the realm of science fiction, has rapidly evolved into a powerful force driving innovation across industries. From machine learning algorithms to natural language processing techniques, AI encompasses a broad spectrum of technologies that enable machines to learn from data, adapt to changing environments, and perform tasks traditionally reserved for human intelligence.

The Evolution of Marketing:

Marketing, too, has undergone a profound transformation in the digital age, as businesses grapple with the complexities of an interconnected, data-driven world. Traditional marketing approaches, characterized by mass media campaigns and one-size-fits-all messaging, have given way to more personalized, data-driven strategies that prioritize consumer engagement, relevance, and authenticity.

The Promise of AI in Marketing:

Against this backdrop, AI has emerged as a game-changer for marketers seeking to navigate the complexities of modern marketing landscapes. By harnessing the power of AI-driven analytics, machine learning algorithms, and predictive modeling techniques, marketers can unlock valuable insights from vast amounts of data, anticipate consumer behavior, and tailor marketing strategies to individual preferences and preferences.

Applications of AI in Marketing:

The applications of AI in marketing are diverse and far-reaching, spanning across various stages of the customer journey. From customer segmentation and targeting to content optimization and campaign automation, AI-powered technologies enable marketers to streamline processes, enhance decision-making, and deliver personalized experiences that resonate with target audiences.

Ethical and Privacy Considerations:

However, the widespread adoption of AI in marketing also raises important ethical and privacy considerations. As AI algorithms become increasingly sophisticated in analyzing consumer data and predicting behavior, marketers must prioritize transparency, accountability, and data privacy to maintain consumer trust and safeguard against potential misuse of personal information.

The Road Ahead:

As we embark on a journey into the realm of AI-driven marketing, it is essential to recognize both the opportunities and challenges that lie ahead. By embracing AI technologies responsibly, marketers can harness the transformative power of AI to drive innovation, foster meaningful connections with consumers, and unlock new opportunities for growth and success in the dynamic world of global trend marketing.

Applications of AI in Identifying and Analyzing Trends

Artificial Intelligence (AI) has revolutionized the way businesses identify and analyze trends in the global marketplace, providing marketers with powerful tools and techniques to gain insights, predict future developments, and capitalize on emerging opportunities. The applications of AI in identifying and analyzing trends are diverse and multifaceted, spanning across various domains of marketing and consumer behavior. The following are key applications of AI in this context:

Data Mining and Pattern Recognition:

AI-powered algorithms excel at data mining and pattern recognition, enabling marketers to uncover hidden insights and correlations within large datasets. By analyzing diverse sources of data, including social media conversations, online search trends, consumer reviews, and market research reports, AI algorithms can identify patterns, anomalies, and emerging trends that may not be immediately apparent to human analysts.

Natural Language Processing (NLP): Natural language processing (NLP) techniques enable AI systems to understand, interpret, and extract insights from human language data, including text, speech, and sentiment analysis. NLP algorithms can analyze consumer conversations on social media platforms, identify key topics and themes, and gauge sentiment and attitudes towards brands, products, and industry trends in real-time.

Predictive Analytics: AI-powered predictive analytics models enable marketers to forecast future trends and anticipate consumer behavior with a high degree of accuracy. By analyzing historical data, identifying patterns, and leveraging machine learning algorithms, predictive analytics can help marketers predict market trends, demand fluctuations, and consumer preferences, enabling them to proactively adjust their strategies and capitalize on emerging opportunities.

Image and Video Analysis: AI-driven image and video analysis

technologies enable marketers to analyze visual content, including images, videos, and infographics, to uncover trends and insights. By leveraging computer vision algorithms, AI systems can identify visual elements, objects, and trends within multimedia content, helping marketers understand consumer preferences, visual aesthetics, and emerging design trends.

Social Media Listening and Monitoring: AI-powered social media listening and monitoring tools enable marketers to track, analyze, and interpret conversations and trends across social media platforms. By monitoring brand mentions, hashtags, and user engagement metrics, AI algorithms can identify emerging topics, trending hashtags, and viral content, providing marketers with valuable insights into consumer sentiment, preferences, and behavior in real-time.

Market Segmentation and Targeting: AI-driven segmentation and targeting techniques enable marketers to identify and segment audiences based on demographic, psychographic, and behavioral attributes. By analyzing

consumer data and clustering individuals into distinct segments, AI algorithms can help marketers identify niche markets, tailor messaging and offers to specific audience segments, and optimize marketing campaigns for maximum relevance and impact.

Competitive Intelligence and Benchmarking:

AI-powered competitive intelligence tools enable marketers to gain insights into competitor strategies, market dynamics, and industry trends. By analyzing competitor activities, monitoring market trends, and benchmarking performance metrics, AI algorithms can help marketers identify whitespace opportunities, assess competitive threats, and refine their strategies to stay ahead of the competition.

Benefits and Challenges of Using AI in Global Trend Marketing

Artificial Intelligence (AI) has emerged as a powerful tool for businesses seeking to navigate the complexities of global trend marketing, offering a wide array of benefits and opportunities to marketers. However, along with its benefits come unique challenges and considerations that must be addressed to maximize its effectiveness and mitigate potential risks. Understanding both the benefits and challenges of using AI in global trend marketing is essential for marketers seeking to harness its full potential. Let's explore these aspects in detail:

Benefits of Using AI in Global Trend Marketing:

Enhanced Insights and Decision-Making: AI-driven analytics and predictive modeling enable marketers to gain deeper insights into consumer behavior, market trends, and competitive dynamics. By analyzing vast amounts of data, AI algorithms can uncover hidden patterns, identify emerging trends, and provide valuable insights that inform strategic decision-making and drive business growth.

Improved Targeting and Personalization: AI-powered segmentation and targeting techniques enable marketers to identify and engage with specific audience segments based on their preferences, behaviors, and demographics. By delivering personalized content, offers, and recommendations, marketers can enhance customer experiences, drive engagement, and foster stronger relationships with their target audiences.

Real-Time Responsiveness: AI enables real-time monitoring and analysis of market trends, consumer sentiment, and competitive activities, allowing marketers to respond rapidly to changing market dynamics and emerging opportunities. By leveraging AI-driven insights, marketers can adapt their strategies, optimize campaigns, and capitalize on trends as they unfold in real-time.

Automation and Efficiency: AI-powered automation streamlines repetitive tasks, enhances operational efficiency, and frees up valuable time and resources for marketers to focus on strategic initiatives. From campaign management and content optimization to customer service and lead nurturing, AI-driven automation enables marketers to scale their efforts and achieve greater productivity and scalability.

Competitive Advantage: Marketers who embrace AI technologies gain a competitive advantage by leveraging advanced analytics, predictive modeling, and automation capabilities to outperform rivals and capture market share. By staying ahead of the curve and leveraging AI-driven insights, marketers can differentiate their brands, drive innovation, and maintain a leadership position in the marketplace.

Challenges of Using AI in Global Trend Marketing:

Data Privacy and Security: AI relies on vast amounts of data to generate insights and make predictions, raising concerns about data privacy, security, and compliance. Marketers must adhere to strict data protection regulations, implement robust security measures, and ensure transparency and accountability in data collection, storage, and usage practices.

Ethical Considerations: The use of AI in marketing raises ethical considerations related to algorithmic bias, discrimination, and fairness. Marketers must be vigilant in monitoring AI algorithms for unintended biases and discriminatory outcomes, and take proactive steps to mitigate biases and ensure equitable treatment of all consumers.

Complexity and Technical Expertise: Implementing AI technologies requires specialized skills, technical expertise, and infrastructure investments that may be challenging for some organizations to acquire and maintain. Marketers must invest in training, talent acquisition, and partnerships with technology vendors to effectively leverage AI and maximize its impact on marketing initiatives.

Integration and Compatibility: Integrating AI technologies with existing marketing systems and workflows can be complex and time-consuming, requiring seamless integration with legacy systems, data sources, and third-party platforms. Marketers must ensure compatibility, interoperability, and scalability of AI solutions to avoid disruptions and maximize ROI.

Overreliance on AI: While AI offers powerful capabilities for analyzing data and generating insights, marketers must guard against overreliance on AI-driven decision-making and maintain a balance between human judgment and machine intelligence. Human oversight and critical thinking are essential for interpreting AI-driven insights, validating predictions, and making informed decisions in complex and uncertain environments.

CHAPTER 3

ANALYZING CURRENT MARKETING TRENDS

In the ever-evolving landscape of global marketing, staying abreast of current trends is essential for businesses seeking to remain competitive, engage with consumers effectively, and drive sustainable growth. Analyzing current marketing trends involves a multifaceted approach that encompasses monitoring industry developments, consumer behaviors, technological innovations, and cultural shifts. In this chapter, we explore the methodologies and best practices for analyzing current marketing trends and leveraging AI-driven insights to gain a competitive edge in the global marketplace.

Data-driven Insights: Data serves as the foundation for analyzing current marketing trends, providing valuable insights into consumer preferences, market dynamics, and competitive landscapes. By leveraging AI-powered analytics tools, marketers can collect, process, and analyze vast amounts of data from diverse sources, including social media platforms, web analytics, market research reports, and customer feedback channels. Data-driven insights enable marketers to identify emerging trends, track consumer sentiment, and measure the effectiveness of marketing campaigns in real-time.

Social Listening and Monitoring:

Social media platforms are valuable sources of real-time data and insights into consumer conversations, opinions, and trends. Social listening and monitoring tools enable marketers to track brand mentions, monitor industry hashtags, and analyze user engagement metrics across various social media channels. By monitoring social media conversations, marketers can identify emerging topics, gauge consumer sentiment, and detect shifts in consumer preferences that may impact marketing strategies.

Trend Analysis and Prediction:

Trend analysis involves examining historical data, identifying patterns, and extrapolating insights to predict future developments in the marketplace. AI-powered predictive analytics models enable marketers to forecast trends, anticipate consumer behavior, and adapt marketing strategies to capitalize on emerging opportunities. By analyzing historical sales data, search trends, and consumer demographics, marketers can identify patterns and correlations that inform strategic decision-making and campaign optimization.

Competitive Intelligence: Analyzing competitors' strategies, market positioning, and performance metrics provides valuable insights into industry trends and emerging opportunities. Competitive intelligence tools enable marketers to monitor competitor activities, benchmark performance metrics, and identify gaps or weaknesses in competitors' offerings. By understanding competitors' strengths and weaknesses, marketers can refine their own strategies, differentiate their brand, and capitalize on competitive opportunities in the marketplace.

Cultural and Societal Trends: Cultural and societal trends influence consumer behaviors, preferences, and purchasing decisions in profound ways.

Analyzing cultural trends, social movements, and demographic shifts enables marketers to understand the underlying motivations and values driving consumer behavior. By staying attuned to cultural nuances, marketers can develop campaigns that resonate with target audiences, foster authentic connections, and address consumers' evolving needs and aspirations.

Technological Innovations:

Technological advancements shape the way businesses interact with consumers, deliver products and services, and communicate brand messages. Analyzing technological innovations, such as AI, augmented reality, and voice search, helps marketers anticipate shifts in consumer behavior and preferences. By embracing emerging technologies, marketers can innovate their marketing strategies, enhance customer experiences, and stay ahead of the curve in an increasingly digital marketplace.

Identifying Emerging Market Trends

In the dynamic landscape of global trend marketing, identifying emerging market trends is essential for businesses seeking to anticipate shifts in consumer behavior, capitalize on new opportunities, and stay ahead of the competition. Emerging market trends encompass a wide range of developments, from technological innovations and cultural shifts to changes in consumer preferences and industry dynamics. In this chapter, we explore the methodologies and best practices for identifying emerging market trends and leveraging AI-driven insights to drive strategic decision-making in the global marketplace.

Data-driven Analysis: Data serves as the foundation for identifying emerging market trends, providing valuable insights into consumer behavior, market dynamics, and competitive landscapes. By leveraging AI-powered analytics tools, marketers can collect, process, and analyze vast amounts of data from diverse sources, including social media platforms, web analytics, market research reports, and customer feedback channels. Data-driven analysis enables marketers to identify patterns, detect anomalies, and uncover emerging trends that may impact the market.

Social Listening and Monitoring:

Social media platforms are valuable sources of real-time data and insights into consumer conversations, opinions, and trends. Social listening and monitoring tools enable marketers to track brand mentions, monitor industry hashtags, and analyze user engagement metrics across various social media channels. By monitoring social media conversations, marketers can identify emerging topics, gauge consumer sentiment, and detect shifts in consumer preferences that may signal emerging market trends.

Trend Forecasting and Prediction:

Trend forecasting involves analyzing historical data, identifying patterns, and extrapolating insights to predict future developments in the marketplace. AI-powered predictive analytics models enable marketers to forecast trends, anticipate consumer behavior, and adapt marketing strategies to capitalize on emerging opportunities. By analyzing historical sales data, search trends, and consumer demographics, marketers can identify patterns and correlations that inform strategic decision-making and campaign optimization.

Industry Research and Competitive Intelligence:

Keeping abreast of industry developments, competitor strategies, and market dynamics is essential for identifying emerging market trends. Industry research reports, competitor analysis, and market intelligence tools provide valuable insights into emerging trends, disruptive technologies, and evolving consumer preferences. By analyzing competitors' strategies, market positioning, and performance metrics, marketers can identify gaps or weaknesses in the market and capitalize on emerging opportunities.

Cultural and Societal Insights:

Cultural and societal trends shape consumer behaviors, preferences, and purchasing decisions in profound ways. Understanding cultural shifts, social movements, and demographic changes enables marketers to identify emerging market trends and adapt their strategies accordingly. By staying attuned to cultural nuances, marketers can develop campaigns that resonate with target audiences, foster authentic connections, and address consumers' evolving needs and aspirations.

Technological Innovations and Disruptions:

Technological advancements drive innovation and shape the way businesses interact with consumers and deliver products and services. Monitoring technological innovations and disruptions helps marketers anticipate shifts in consumer behavior and preferences. By embracing emerging technologies such as AI, augmented reality, and blockchain, marketers can innovate their marketing strategies, enhance customer experiences, and capitalize on emerging trends in the global marketplace.

Case Studies on Successful Trend Identification and Utilization

Nike's Adaptation to Athleisure Trend: Nike, a global leader in athletic footwear and apparel, successfully identified and capitalized on the athleisure trend through data-driven insights and consumer research. By leveraging AI-powered analytics tools to analyze social media conversations, search trends, and consumer behavior patterns, Nike recognized the growing demand for comfortable, versatile activewear that could transition seamlessly from the gym to everyday wear. Nike's innovative product offerings, such as the Tech Fleece collection and Nike Flyknit sneakers, catered to consumers seeking functional yet stylish athletic wear. Through targeted marketing campaigns and strategic partnerships with influencers, Nike positioned itself as a trendsetter in the athleisure market, driving sales and brand loyalty among fitness enthusiasts and fashion-conscious consumers alike.

Starbucks' Embrace of Plant-Based Trends: Starbucks, a global coffeehouse chain, successfully identified and embraced the plant-based trend by introducing dairy-free milk alternatives and plant-based menu options in response to shifting consumer preferences. By leveraging AI-driven customer feedback analysis and trend monitoring tools, Starbucks identified a growing demand for plant-based beverages and food items among health-conscious consumers and those with dietary restrictions. Starbucks' strategic collaboration with alternative milk suppliers and innovative menu offerings, such as the Coconutmilk Latte and Beyond Meat Breakfast Sandwich, resonated with consumers seeking healthier, environmentally sustainable options. Through targeted marketing campaigns and social media engagement, Starbucks effectively communicated its commitment to sustainability and catered to evolving consumer tastes, driving sales and reinforcing its position as a leader in the coffee industry.

Amazon's Expansion into Smart Home Technology: Amazon, a global e-commerce giant, successfully identified and capitalized on the emerging trend of smart home technology through strategic acquisitions and product innovation. Recognizing the growing popularity of connected devices and voice-activated assistants, Amazon acquired smart home technology companies such as Ring and Blink to expand its product portfolio and enhance its ecosystem of Alexa-enabled devices. Leveraging AI-driven consumer insights and market research, Amazon identified key pain points and consumer preferences in the smart home market, leading to the development of products like the Amazon Echo and Ring Video Doorbell. Through targeted marketing efforts and cross-promotion across its platforms, Amazon positioned itself as a leader in the smart home industry, driving adoption and consumer engagement while capturing market share from competitors.

Lululemon's Expansion into Wellness and Lifestyle: Lululemon, a leading athletic apparel brand, successfully identified and capitalized on the emerging trend of wellness and lifestyle by expanding its product offerings beyond traditional activewear. Leveraging AI-powered data analytics and consumer behavior insights, Lululemon recognized a shift in consumer preferences towards holistic wellness and self-care practices. In response, Lululemon expanded its product range to include yoga accessories, meditation essentials, and lifestyle apparel designed for both athletic performance and everyday wear. Through strategic partnerships with wellness influencers and experiential marketing initiatives, Lululemon cultivated a lifestyle brand image that resonated with health-conscious consumers seeking balance and mindfulness in their daily lives. By staying attuned to emerging trends and consumer preferences, Lululemon strengthened its brand identity and diversified its revenue streams, driving growth and differentiation in the competitive activewear market.

Data Analysis Techniques and Tools for Trend Evaluation

In the realm of global trend marketing, data analysis serves as a cornerstone for evaluating trends, uncovering insights, and making informed strategic decisions. Leveraging advanced data analysis techniques and tools empowers marketers to navigate the complexities of the marketplace, anticipate shifts in consumer behavior, and capitalize on emerging opportunities. In this chapter, we explore key data analysis techniques and tools essential for trend evaluation in the context of global trend marketing:

Descriptive Analytics: Descriptive analytics involves analyzing historical data to understand past trends, patterns, and performance metrics. By examining key indicators such as sales figures, website traffic, and social media engagement metrics, marketers can gain insights into past trends and consumer behaviors. Descriptive analytics provides a foundation for trend evaluation by establishing

baseline metrics and identifying areas of opportunity or improvement.

Predictive Analytics: Predictive analytics utilizes statistical algorithms and machine learning techniques to forecast future trends and anticipate changes in consumer behavior. By analyzing historical data and identifying patterns, predictive analytics models can predict future outcomes, such as sales forecasts, demand fluctuations, and consumer preferences. Predictive analytics empowers marketers to anticipate emerging trends, optimize marketing strategies, and allocate resources effectively to capitalize on future opportunities.

Social Media Analytics: Social media analytics tools enable marketers to monitor and analyze conversations, trends, and user engagement metrics across various social media platforms. By tracking brand mentions, hashtags, and user sentiment, social media analytics provide insights into consumer preferences, emerging topics, and viral trends in real-time. Social media analytics tools such as Sprout Social, Hootsuite, and Brandwatch enable marketers to measure the impact of their social media campaigns, identify influencers, and engage with consumers effectively.

Web Analytics:

Web analytics tools, such as Google Analytics and Adobe Analytics, enable marketers to track website traffic, user behavior, and conversion metrics. By analyzing website traffic sources, page views, and user engagement metrics, marketers can gain insights into consumer preferences, content effectiveness, and conversion pathways. Web analytics tools provide valuable data for evaluating the performance of marketing campaigns, optimizing website content, and improving the user experience to drive conversions and engagement.

Text Analytics:

Text analytics techniques enable marketers to analyze unstructured text data, such as customer reviews, social media posts, and online forums, to uncover insights and trends. Natural language processing (NLP) algorithms extract meaningful information from textual data, including sentiment analysis, topic modeling, and keyword extraction. Text analytics tools enable marketers to identify emerging topics, sentiment trends, and consumer preferences, providing valuable insights for trend evaluation and strategic decision-making.

Data Visualization Tools:

Data visualization tools, such as Tableau, Power BI, and Google Data Studio, enable marketers to visualize trends, patterns, and insights from complex datasets. By creating interactive dashboards, charts, and graphs, data visualization tools facilitate data exploration and communication of insights to stakeholders. Data visualization enhances the effectiveness of trend evaluation by providing intuitive visual representations of key metrics and trends, enabling marketers to identify patterns and make data-driven decisions.

Market Research Surveys and Panels:

Market research surveys and panels provide valuable qualitative and quantitative data for trend evaluation and consumer insights. By collecting feedback from target audiences through surveys, focus groups, and online panels, marketers can gain insights into consumer preferences, attitudes, and behaviors. Market research surveys enable marketers to validate hypotheses, test concepts, and uncover unmet needs, providing valuable input for trend evaluation and strategic planning.

CHAPTER 4

IMPLEMENTING GLOBAL TREND MARKETING STRATEGIES

Implementing global trend marketing strategies requires a strategic approach that integrates data-driven insights, market intelligence, and innovative tactics to capitalize on emerging trends and consumer preferences. In this chapter, we explore the key principles and best practices for implementing effective global trend marketing strategies leveraging AI-driven methodologies and tools.

Data-Driven Decision Making:

Data serves as the foundation for effective global trend marketing strategies. By leveraging AI-driven analytics tools, marketers can collect, analyze, and interpret vast amounts of data from diverse sources to uncover insights into consumer behavior, market trends, and competitive landscapes. Through data-driven decision-making processes, marketers can identify emerging trends, evaluate market opportunities, and optimize marketing strategies to resonate with target audiences across diverse global markets.

Market Segmentation and Targeting:

Understanding the diverse needs, preferences, and behaviors of global consumers is essential for successful trend marketing strategies. By segmenting target audiences based on demographic, psychographic, and behavioral attributes, marketers can tailor messaging, offers, and experiences to resonate with specific consumer segments. AI-powered segmentation techniques enable marketers to identify micro-segments and personalize marketing efforts at scale, driving engagement and conversion rates across global markets.

Cultural Sensitivity and Localization:

Cultural nuances and regional differences play a significant role in shaping consumer perceptions and behaviors across global markets. Marketers must adapt their messaging, imagery, and branding strategies to align with local customs, languages, and cultural sensitivities. AI-driven sentiment analysis and language processing tools enable marketers to understand cultural nuances, localize content, and foster authentic connections with diverse audiences, enhancing brand relevance and resonance in global markets.

Agile and Responsive Campaign Execution:

In the fast-paced world of global trend marketing, agility and responsiveness are key to staying ahead of the curve. Marketers must be prepared to adapt their strategies quickly in response to changing market dynamics, emerging trends, and competitive threats. By leveraging AI-powered predictive analytics and real-time monitoring tools, marketers can track campaign performance, identify optimization opportunities, and adjust strategies on the fly to maximize impact and ROI.

Cross-Channel Integration and Optimization:

Consumers engage with brands across multiple touchpoints and channels, from social media platforms and search engines to e-commerce websites and offline stores. Marketers must adopt a holistic approach to global trend marketing that integrates messaging, content, and experiences seamlessly across all channels. AI-driven attribution modeling and cross-channel optimization techniques enable marketers to understand the customer journey, allocate resources effectively, and optimize marketing spend to drive maximum impact and conversion across global markets.

Continuous Learning and Innovation:

The landscape of global trend marketing is constantly evolving, driven by technological advancements, shifting consumer preferences, and emerging market trends. Marketers must foster a culture of continuous learning, experimentation, and innovation to stay ahead of the curve and capitalize on new opportunities. By leveraging AI-driven insights and industry benchmarks, marketers can identify areas for improvement, test new strategies, and iterate on campaigns to drive innovation and achieve sustainable growth in the dynamic global marketplace.

Developing Strategies Based on Identified Trends

Identifying trends is only the first step in the process of effective global trend marketing. Once trends are recognized, businesses must develop comprehensive strategies to capitalize on these trends and align their marketing efforts with evolving consumer preferences. In this chapter, we explore the key principles and best practices for developing strategies based on identified trends using AI-driven methodologies and insights.

Trend Analysis and Interpretation: Before developing strategies, it's essential to conduct in-depth analysis and interpretation of identified trends. AI-powered analytics tools can help businesses understand the underlying drivers, implications, and potential impact of trends on their target markets. By analyzing historical data, consumer behavior patterns, and market dynamics, businesses can gain insights into the longevity and sustainability of trends, enabling informed decision-making and strategic planning.

Market Segmentation and Targeting:

Once trends are identified, businesses must segment their target markets and tailor their strategies to resonate with specific audience segments. AI-driven segmentation techniques enable businesses to categorize consumers based on demographic, psychographic, and behavioral attributes, allowing for personalized messaging and offers. By targeting niche segments with tailored content and experiences, businesses can enhance engagement, foster brand loyalty, and drive conversion rates.

Product and Service Innovation:

Trends often create opportunities for product and service innovation that meet evolving consumer needs and preferences. By leveraging AI-driven insights and consumer feedback, businesses can identify gaps in the market and develop innovative offerings that address emerging trends. Whether it's introducing new product features, expanding product lines, or launching entirely new offerings, businesses can stay ahead of the competition and capture market share by aligning their offerings with identified trends.

Content and Messaging Strategy:

Crafting compelling content and messaging that resonates with target audiences is critical for effective trend marketing. Businesses must develop content that speaks to consumer interests, values, and aspirations, aligning with identified trends and market preferences. AI-driven content analysis tools can help businesses understand which types of content perform best with their target audiences, enabling them to optimize messaging strategies and drive engagement across digital channels.

Channel Optimization and Distribution:

Effective trend marketing requires businesses to deliver their messages through the right channels at the right time. By leveraging AI-driven attribution modeling and cross-channel optimization techniques, businesses can identify the most effective channels for reaching their target audiences and allocate resources accordingly. Whether it's social media platforms, search engines, email marketing, or offline channels, businesses must optimize their distribution strategies to maximize reach and impact.

Measurement and Optimization:

Continuous measurement and optimization are essential for refining and improving trend marketing strategies over time. Businesses must establish key performance indicators (KPIs) and leverage AI-powered analytics tools to track and analyze campaign performance against predefined goals. By monitoring metrics such as engagement rates, conversion rates, and return on investment (ROI), businesses can identify areas for improvement, optimize campaigns in real-time, and drive continuous improvement in their trend marketing efforts.

Leveraging AI-Powered Tools and Platforms

In the realm of global trend marketing, the integration of artificial intelligence (AI) has revolutionized the way businesses analyze data, understand consumer behavior, and capitalize on emerging trends. AI-powered tools and platforms offer marketers unprecedented capabilities to extract insights, optimize campaigns, and drive strategic decision-making in the dynamic landscape of global trend marketing. In this chapter, we explore the various ways businesses can leverage AI-powered tools and platforms to enhance their marketing strategies and stay ahead of the curve.

Data Analytics and Insights: AI-powered data analytics tools enable businesses to analyze vast amounts of structured and unstructured data from diverse sources, including social media platforms, customer interactions, and market trends. By leveraging machine learning algorithms and natural language processing techniques, businesses can extract actionable insights, identify patterns, and uncover hidden trends within their datasets. These insights empower marketers to make informed decisions, optimize campaigns, and tailor strategies to meet evolving consumer preferences and market dynamics.

Predictive Analytics and Forecasting: Predictive analytics platforms leverage AI algorithms to forecast future trends, anticipate consumer behavior, and identify potential opportunities and risks. By analyzing historical data and identifying patterns, predictive analytics models can provide businesses with valuable insights into market trends, demand fluctuations, and competitive dynamics. This enables marketers to proactively adjust their strategies, allocate resources effectively, and capitalize on emerging opportunities before they become mainstream.

Consumer Segmentation and Personalization:

AI-powered segmentation and personalization tools enable businesses to divide their target audience into distinct segments based on demographic, psychographic, and behavioral attributes. By understanding the unique preferences and needs of each segment, marketers can deliver personalized experiences, tailored recommendations, and targeted messaging that resonate with individual consumers. This level of personalization enhances customer engagement, fosters brand loyalty, and drives conversion rates across various marketing channels.

Content Creation and Optimization:

AI-driven content creation platforms leverage natural language processing (NLP) and machine learning algorithms to generate high-quality, engaging content at scale. From blog posts and social media captions to email newsletters and product descriptions, AI-powered content creation tools enable marketers to produce relevant, compelling content that resonates with their target audience. Additionally, AI-driven content optimization platforms help businesses analyze content performance, identify optimization opportunities, and refine their content strategies to maximize engagement and impact.

Adaptive Campaign Management:

AI-powered campaign management platforms enable businesses to optimize their marketing campaigns in real-time, based on dynamic market conditions and consumer behavior. By leveraging predictive analytics and machine learning algorithms, these platforms can automatically adjust campaign parameters, allocate budgets, and optimize targeting criteria to maximize ROI and drive business outcomes. This level of automation and adaptability allows marketers to stay agile, respond quickly to changes, and continuously optimize their campaigns for maximum effectiveness.

Sentiment Analysis and Social Listening:

AI-powered sentiment analysis and social listening tools enable businesses to monitor brand mentions, track consumer sentiment, and analyze conversations across social media platforms and online forums. By understanding how consumers perceive their brand and products, businesses can identify areas for improvement, address customer concerns, and capitalize on positive sentiment to enhance brand reputation and loyalty. Additionally, sentiment analysis enables businesses to identify emerging trends, detect potential crises, and proactively manage their online presence in real-time.

Integrating Trend Marketing with Overall Marketing Strategy

In the complex landscape of modern marketing, integrating trend marketing with an overarching marketing strategy is crucial for businesses aiming to stay relevant, competitive, and responsive to evolving consumer preferences. Trend marketing, when seamlessly integrated into the broader marketing strategy, enables businesses to capitalize on emerging opportunities, foster consumer engagement, and drive sustainable growth. In this chapter, we explore the key principles and best practices for integrating trend marketing with the overall marketing strategy, leveraging AI-driven methodologies and insights.

Aligning with Brand Values and Identity:

Trend marketing initiatives should align closely with the brand's core values, mission, and identity. By integrating trend marketing efforts with the overall brand strategy, businesses can ensure consistency, authenticity, and alignment with their brand ethos. AI-powered

82

sentiment analysis and brand monitoring tools enable businesses to gauge consumer perceptions, identify alignment opportunities, and tailor trend marketing campaigns to resonate with their brand identity, fostering stronger connections with target audiences.

Strategic Planning and Goal Setting:
Integrating trend marketing into the overall marketing strategy requires strategic planning and goal setting to ensure alignment with broader business objectives. By defining clear goals, KPIs, and success metrics, businesses can measure the effectiveness of trend marketing initiatives and track their impact on key business outcomes. AI-driven predictive analytics and forecasting tools enable businesses to anticipate trends, set achievable targets, and allocate resources effectively to maximize the ROI of trend marketing efforts.

Audience Segmentation and Targeting:
Effective trend marketing relies on precise audience segmentation and targeting strategies to reach the right consumers with the right message at the

right time. By leveraging AI-powered segmentation techniques, businesses can divide their target audience into distinct segments based on demographic, psychographic, and behavioral attributes. This enables marketers to tailor trend marketing campaigns to specific audience segments, delivering personalized experiences that resonate with individual consumer preferences and interests.

Content Creation and Distribution:

Integrating trend marketing with the overall content strategy involves creating compelling, relevant content that captures the essence of emerging trends while staying true to the brand's voice and narrative. AI-powered content creation platforms enable businesses to generate high-quality, engaging content at scale, leveraging natural language processing and machine learning algorithms to craft personalized messaging that resonates with target audiences. By strategically distributing content across multiple channels, businesses can amplify their reach, drive engagement, and maximize the impact of trend marketing campaigns.

Continuous Monitoring and Optimization: Trend marketing is an iterative process that requires continuous monitoring, analysis, and optimization to stay ahead of evolving consumer preferences and market dynamics. By leveraging AI-driven analytics and real-time monitoring tools, businesses can track the performance of trend marketing initiatives, identify optimization opportunities, and adapt their strategies in response to changing trends and consumer behavior patterns. This enables marketers to stay agile, responsive, and proactive in optimizing trend marketing campaigns for maximum impact and effectiveness.

Measuring Impact and ROI: Integrating trend marketing with the overall marketing strategy necessitates measuring the impact and ROI of trend marketing initiatives to justify investment and inform future decision-making. By leveraging AI-powered attribution modeling and performance analytics, businesses can attribute conversions, engagement, and revenue back to specific trend marketing efforts, enabling them to assess effectiveness, identify areas for improvement, and optimize resource allocation for maximum ROI.

CHAPTER 5

ADAPTING TO CHANGING MARKET TRENDS

In the fast-paced and dynamic landscape of global trend marketing, businesses must possess the agility and foresight to adapt to changing market trends swiftly and effectively. The ability to recognize, analyze, and respond to emerging trends is essential for maintaining relevance, capturing opportunities, and sustaining competitive advantage. In this chapter, we explore the principles and strategies for adapting to changing market trends, leveraging AI-driven insights and methodologies to navigate the complexities of the global marketplace.

Continuous Monitoring and Analysis: Adapting to changing market trends begins with continuous monitoring and analysis of market dynamics, consumer behavior, and competitive landscapes. By leveraging AI-powered analytics tools, businesses can collect, process, and analyze vast amounts of data from diverse sources, including social media platforms, consumer reviews, market research reports, and industry publications. This enables businesses to identify emerging trends, anticipate shifts in consumer preferences, and proactively adjust their strategies to stay ahead of the curve.

Agile Decision-Making Processes: Adapting to changing market trends requires agile decision-making processes that enable businesses to respond quickly and decisively to evolving market conditions. By decentralizing decision-making authority, empowering cross-functional teams, and fostering a culture of experimentation and innovation, businesses can accelerate the pace of adaptation and capitalize on emerging opportunities. AI-driven predictive analytics and scenario modeling tools enable businesses to simulate various scenarios, evaluate potential outcomes, and make informed decisions based on data-driven insights.

Flexibility and Scalability: Adapting to changing market trends requires flexibility and scalability in organizational structures, processes, and resources. Businesses must be prepared to reallocate resources, pivot strategies, and scale initiatives in response to shifting market dynamics and emerging opportunities. By leveraging cloud-based infrastructure, automation tools, and flexible workforce models, businesses can adapt to changing demands, optimize resource utilization, and maintain operational efficiency in the face of uncertainty.

Customer-Centric Approach:

Adapting to changing market trends necessitates a customer-centric approach that prioritizes understanding and meeting the evolving needs, preferences, and expectations of target audiences. By leveraging AI-powered segmentation and personalization techniques, businesses can tailor products, services, and messaging to resonate with specific audience segments, driving engagement and loyalty. Continuous feedback loops, customer surveys, and sentiment analysis tools enable businesses to gather insights into customer sentiment, preferences, and pain points, informing iterative improvements and adaptation strategies.

Strategic Partnerships and Collaboration:

Adapting to changing market trends often requires collaboration and partnerships with external stakeholders, including suppliers, distributors, industry associations, and technology providers. Strategic alliances enable businesses to access complementary resources, expertise, and networks, expanding their reach and capabilities in the marketplace. AI-driven analytics and predictive modeling tools facilitate partner identification, evaluation, and collaboration, enabling businesses to forge mutually beneficial relationships that drive innovation and value creation.

Learning and Innovation:

Adapting to changing market trends is an ongoing learning process that requires a commitment to innovation, experimentation, and continuous improvement. By fostering a culture of curiosity, creativity, and learning, businesses can encourage employees to explore new ideas, challenge assumptions, and embrace change. AI-driven knowledge management systems, training programs, and innovation hubs enable businesses to capture and disseminate best practices, share insights, and cultivate a culture of innovation that fuels adaptation and growth in the face of changing market dynamics.

Monitoring and Tracking Trends in Real-Time

In the fast-paced world of global trend marketing, the ability to monitor and track trends in real-time is essential for businesses seeking to stay ahead of the curve, adapt to evolving consumer preferences, and capitalize on emerging opportunities. Real-time monitoring enables businesses to gather timely insights, identify patterns, and make informed decisions that drive strategic outcomes. In this chapter, we explore the principles and strategies for monitoring and tracking trends in real-time, leveraging AI-powered methodologies and technologies to navigate the complexities of the global marketplace.

Data Aggregation and Integration: Real-time trend monitoring begins with the aggregation and integration of data from diverse sources, including social media platforms, online forums, news websites, industry publications, and consumer feedback channels. By leveraging AI-powered data aggregation tools, businesses can collect and consolidate real-time data streams into centralized repositories, enabling comprehensive trend analysis and insight generation.

Social Media Listening and Sentiment Analysis: Social media platforms serve as valuable sources of real-time data and insights into consumer conversations, opinions, and behaviors. By leveraging AI-driven social media listening and sentiment analysis tools, businesses can monitor brand mentions, track trending topics, and analyze consumer sentiment in real-time. This enables businesses to detect emerging trends, gauge consumer reactions to marketing campaigns, and identify potential opportunities or threats to their brand reputation.

Search Engine Trends and Keyword Analysis: Search engines offer valuable insights into consumer interests, preferences, and intent. By monitoring search engine trends and conducting keyword analysis in real-time, businesses can identify trending topics, popular search queries, and emerging keywords related to their industry or niche. AI-powered search analytics tools enable businesses to track changes in search volume, identify rising search trends, and optimize content strategies to capitalize on relevant search queries and drive organic traffic to their websites.

Web Analytics and User Behavior Tracking: Web analytics platforms provide valuable insights into user behavior, engagement patterns, and conversion metrics on websites and digital platforms. By leveraging AI-driven web analytics tools, businesses can track real-time metrics such as website traffic, bounce rates, session durations, and conversion rates. This enables businesses to identify performance trends, optimize user experiences, and make data-driven decisions to enhance website performance and drive desired outcomes.

Market Intelligence and Competitor Analysis:

Real-time monitoring of market intelligence and competitor activities is essential for staying informed about industry trends, competitive landscapes, and market dynamics. AI-powered competitive intelligence tools enable businesses to track competitor strategies, monitor product launches, and analyze market positioning in real-time. By identifying gaps or weaknesses in competitors' offerings and capitalizing on emerging opportunities, businesses can gain a competitive edge and position themselves for success in the marketplace.

Predictive Analytics and Forecasting:

Real-time trend monitoring is enhanced by predictive analytics and forecasting capabilities that enable businesses to anticipate future trends and market developments. By leveraging AI-driven predictive models and machine learning algorithms, businesses can analyze historical data, identify patterns, and forecast future trends with a high degree of accuracy. This enables businesses to proactively adjust their strategies, allocate resources effectively, and capitalize on emerging opportunities before they become mainstream.

Flexibility and Agility in Marketing Strategies

In the ever-evolving landscape of global trend marketing, flexibility and agility are essential attributes for businesses aiming to navigate through dynamic market conditions, capitalize on emerging opportunities, and maintain a competitive edge. Flexibility allows businesses to adapt their strategies to changing trends and consumer preferences, while agility enables swift and responsive actions in the face of evolving market dynamics. In this chapter, we delve into the significance of flexibility and agility in marketing strategies, exploring how businesses can leverage these attributes to drive success in the global marketplace.

Adaptation to Changing Trends:

Flexibility in marketing strategies involves the ability to adapt to changing market trends, consumer behaviors, and competitive landscapes. By staying attuned to emerging trends and consumer preferences, businesses can adjust their marketing strategies accordingly to remain relevant and resonate with their target audience. Flexibility allows businesses to pivot quickly, experiment with new approaches, and capitalize on emerging opportunities that align with their brand identity and objectives.

Responsive Decision-Making Processes:

Agility in marketing strategies entails responsive decision-making processes that enable businesses to react swiftly to evolving market dynamics and consumer needs. By empowering cross-functional teams, fostering a culture of innovation, and decentralizing decision-making authority, businesses can expedite the pace of decision-making and implementation. Agile decision-making enables businesses to seize opportunities, mitigate risks, and adapt strategies in real-time to achieve desired outcomes and drive business growth.

Iterative Experimentation and Optimization: Flexibility and agility in marketing strategies facilitate iterative experimentation and optimization processes that enable continuous improvement and innovation. By embracing a test-and-learn mindset, businesses can experiment with new ideas, campaigns, and tactics to gauge their effectiveness and refine their strategies based on performance feedback. Agile optimization enables businesses to iterate rapidly, identify optimization opportunities, and adapt strategies to maximize ROI and drive sustainable growth in the competitive marketplace.

Cross-Functional Collaboration and Integration: Flexibility and agility in marketing strategies require cross-functional collaboration and integration across departments, teams, and business units. By breaking down silos, fostering collaboration, and promoting knowledge sharing, businesses can leverage diverse perspectives and expertise to develop holistic marketing strategies that align with broader business objectives. Cross-functional integration enables businesses to synchronize efforts, streamline processes, and drive alignment across marketing, sales, product development, and customer service functions.

Data-Driven Decision-Making and Insights:

Flexibility and agility in marketing strategies are bolstered by data-driven decision-making processes and insights that enable businesses to make informed decisions and optimize performance. By leveraging AI-driven analytics tools, businesses can gather, analyze, and interpret vast amounts of data from diverse sources to uncover actionable insights, identify trends, and anticipate consumer behavior. Data-driven decision-making enables businesses to adapt strategies based on real-time insights, optimize resource allocation, and maximize the impact of marketing initiatives on business outcomes.

Risk Management and Contingency Planning:

Flexibility and agility in marketing strategies entail effective risk management and contingency planning processes that enable businesses to anticipate and mitigate potential challenges and disruptions. By conducting scenario planning, assessing risk factors, and developing contingency plans, businesses can prepare for unexpected events and respond proactively to mitigate their impact on marketing initiatives. Effective risk management enables businesses to maintain operational continuity, safeguard brand reputation, and navigate through uncertainty with resilience and confidence.

Case Studies on Adapting to Shifting Trends

Netflix: Embracing Streaming Trends

As the entertainment industry shifted towards digital streaming, Netflix demonstrated remarkable agility in adapting to shifting trends. Recognizing the growing consumer preference for on-demand content and streaming services, Netflix transitioned from a DVD rental service to a leading global streaming platform. Leveraging AI-powered algorithms, Netflix analyzed user viewing patterns, preferences, and feedback to personalize content recommendations and optimize user experiences. By investing in original content production and global expansion, Netflix capitalized on the rising popularity of streaming platforms, solidifying its position as a dominant player in the digital entertainment landscape.

Adidas: Embracing Sustainable Fashion

With increasing consumer awareness about environmental sustainability, Adidas demonstrated flexibility in adapting its marketing strategies to embrace sustainable fashion trends. Recognizing the growing demand for eco-friendly products and ethical manufacturing practices, Adidas introduced the "Parley for the Oceans" initiative, which repurposed marine plastic waste into sportswear and footwear. By leveraging AI-driven consumer insights and trend analysis, Adidas identified shifting consumer preferences towards sustainable and ethically produced goods. Through strategic partnerships, innovative product designs, and transparent communication, Adidas successfully aligned its brand values with emerging sustainability trends, appealing to environmentally conscious consumers and driving positive brand perception.

Tesla: Leading the Electric Vehicle Revolution

As concerns over climate change and environmental sustainability intensified, Tesla demonstrated unparalleled adaptability in capitalizing on the emerging trend towards electric vehicles (EVs). Leveraging AI-driven research and development, Tesla pioneered advancements in electric vehicle technology, driving innovation and disrupting the automotive industry. By focusing on performance, range, and design, Tesla positioned itself as a leader in the EV market, appealing to environmentally conscious consumers and tech enthusiasts alike. Through strategic marketing campaigns, innovative product launches, and a direct-to-consumer sales model, Tesla challenged traditional automotive manufacturers and accelerated the adoption of electric vehicles worldwide.

Lush Cosmetics: Embracing Conscious Consumerism

With the rise of conscious consumerism and ethical purchasing behavior, Lush Cosmetics demonstrated agility in adapting its marketing strategies to align with shifting trends. Recognizing growing consumer demand for natural, cruelty-free, and ethically sourced beauty products, Lush emphasized transparency, sustainability, and activism in its brand messaging and product offerings. By leveraging social media platforms and user-generated content, Lush engaged with its community of environmentally conscious consumers, fostering authentic connections and driving advocacy for social and environmental causes. Through continuous innovation, product diversification, and customer engagement, Lush maintained its position as a leader in the ethical beauty industry, resonating with consumers who prioritize values-aligned purchasing decisions.

CHAPTER 6

ETHICAL AND PRIVACY CONSIDERATIONS IN AI-DRIVEN MARKETING

As businesses increasingly rely on AI-driven methodologies and technologies to enhance their marketing strategies, it is imperative to address ethical and privacy considerations to ensure responsible and sustainable practices. In the pursuit of leveraging AI for trend marketing, businesses must prioritize consumer trust, data protection, and ethical decision-making. In this chapter, we explore the ethical and privacy considerations associated with AI-driven marketing strategies and provide guidelines for ethical implementation.

Consumer Privacy Protection:

One of the primary ethical considerations in AI-driven marketing is the protection of consumer privacy rights. Businesses must adhere to data protection regulations such as the General Data Protection Regulation (GDPR) and the California Consumer

103

Privacy Act (CCPA) to safeguard consumer data from unauthorized access, use, or disclosure. Transparency in data collection practices, obtaining explicit consent from consumers, and implementing robust security measures are essential for maintaining consumer trust and compliance with privacy regulations.

Data Bias and Fairness: AI algorithms are susceptible to biases inherent in the data used for training, which can perpetuate discrimination and inequality in marketing practices. Businesses must proactively address biases in AI models by ensuring diverse and representative datasets, conducting regular audits of algorithmic decision-making processes, and implementing fairness-aware algorithms. By promoting fairness and inclusivity in AI-driven marketing strategies, businesses can mitigate the risk of unintentional harm and build trust with diverse consumer demographics.

Algorithmic Transparency and Accountability: Transparency in AI-driven marketing practices is essential for building consumer trust and understanding how algorithmic decisions impact their experiences and choices. Businesses should strive for transparency in algorithmic processes, disclose the use of AI technologies in marketing campaigns, and provide consumers with meaningful insights into how their data is utilized for personalized targeting and recommendations. Establishing mechanisms for accountability, auditing algorithmic decision-making, and enabling recourse for consumers in case of algorithmic errors or biases are critical for fostering transparency and accountability in AI-driven marketing practices.

Informed Consent and Consumer Autonomy:

Respecting consumer autonomy and providing informed consent are fundamental principles of ethical marketing practices. Businesses should empower consumers with clear, concise information about how their data will be used for AI-driven marketing purposes, including personalized targeting, recommendation algorithms, and behavioral profiling. Providing consumers with control over their data through opt-in/opt-out mechanisms, granular privacy settings, and preferences management tools enables individuals to make informed choices and exercise autonomy over their personal information.

Mitigating Unintended Consequences:

AI-driven marketing strategies have the potential to produce unintended consequences, including filter bubbles, echo chambers, and algorithmic manipulation. Businesses must anticipate and mitigate these risks by promoting diversity of viewpoints, fostering critical thinking skills, and providing consumers with access to balanced and diverse content. Collaborating with regulators, industry stakeholders, and civil society organizations to develop guidelines, standards, and best practices for ethical AI-driven marketing can help mitigate the negative impacts and promote responsible use of AI technologies in marketing strategies.

Ensuring Data Privacy and Security

In the era of AI-driven marketing strategies, ensuring data privacy and security is paramount to maintain consumer trust, comply with regulations, and mitigate the risks associated with handling sensitive information. As businesses leverage AI technologies to analyze vast amounts of data for trend marketing, they must prioritize robust data privacy and security measures. In this chapter, we explore the principles and best practices for ensuring data privacy and security in the context of global trend marketing strategies.

Compliance with Data Protection Regulations: Businesses must adhere to data protection regulations such as the General Data Protection Regulation (GDPR), the California Consumer Privacy Act (CCPA), and other relevant laws governing data privacy and security. Compliance with these regulations entails obtaining explicit consent from consumers for data collection and processing, providing transparency about data practices, and honoring individuals' rights to access, rectify, or delete their personal information. By aligning with regulatory requirements, businesses demonstrate their commitment

to protecting consumer privacy and upholding legal standards.

Secure Data Storage and Transmission:

Protecting data throughout its lifecycle from collection and storage to transmission and disposal is essential to prevent unauthorized access, data breaches, and cyber threats. Businesses should implement robust encryption protocols, access controls, and data encryption mechanisms to secure sensitive information stored in databases, cloud servers, and third-party platforms. Secure data transmission protocols, such as HTTPS, VPNs, and secure FTP, ensure that data is transmitted securely over networks and protected from interception or unauthorized access.

Data Minimization and Purpose Limitation:

Adopting principles of data minimization and purpose limitation helps mitigate privacy risks and reduce the amount of personal data collected and processed by businesses. Rather than collecting excessive or unnecessary data, businesses should only collect information that is essential for legitimate business purposes and marketing objectives. By limiting data collection to what is strictly necessary and avoiding indiscriminate or speculative data gathering, businesses minimize privacy risks and enhance data protection measures.

Transparency and Consent Management: Transparency in data practices and obtaining informed consent from consumers are foundational principles of data privacy and security. Businesses should provide clear, concise information about their data collection practices, purposes of data processing, and third-party data sharing activities through privacy policies, cookie notices, and consent forms. Implementing user-friendly consent management tools enables consumers to exercise control over their personal information, make informed choices about data sharing preferences, and revoke consent when desired.

Employee Training and Awareness: Human factors play a crucial role in ensuring data privacy and security within organizations. Businesses should invest in comprehensive training programs and awareness initiatives to educate employees about data protection best practices, security protocols, and regulatory compliance requirements. By fostering a culture of data privacy and security awareness, businesses empower employees to recognize and mitigate potential risks, adhere to data handling policies, and maintain vigilance against internal and external threats to data security.

Regular Audits and Compliance Monitoring: Conducting regular audits and compliance monitoring activities helps businesses identify vulnerabilities, assess risk exposure, and ensure ongoing compliance with data protection regulations and industry standards. Internal audits, external assessments, and penetration testing exercises enable businesses to evaluate the effectiveness of security controls, detect potential weaknesses in systems or processes, and implement corrective actions to strengthen data privacy and security posture. By prioritizing continuous improvement and risk management, businesses can proactively address emerging threats and adapt to evolving regulatory requirements in the dynamic landscape of global trend marketing.

Transparency in AI Algorithms and Decision-Making Processes

In the realm of global trend marketing, transparency in AI algorithms and decision-making processes is crucial for fostering consumer trust, promoting accountability, and ensuring ethical and responsible use of AI technologies. As businesses leverage AI-driven methodologies to analyze data, predict trends, and personalize marketing strategies, transparency becomes essential to provide consumers with visibility into how AI algorithms operate and how their data is utilized. In this chapter, we delve into the importance of transparency in AI algorithms and decision-making processes and explore strategies for promoting transparency in the context of global trend marketing strategies.

Understanding AI Algorithms:

Transparency begins with providing consumers with an understanding of the AI algorithms employed in marketing strategies. Businesses should communicate clearly and concisely about the types of algorithms used, their underlying principles, and how they impact decision-making processes. Whether it's machine learning algorithms, natural language processing models, or predictive analytics techniques, consumers should have visibility into how AI algorithms analyze data, generate insights, and drive recommendations in marketing campaigns.

Explanability and Interpretability:
AI algorithms should be designed to be explainable and interpretable, enabling consumers to understand the rationale behind algorithmic decisions and recommendations. Businesses should prioritize the development of AI models that provide transparent explanations for their predictions, classifications, and recommendations. Techniques such as feature importance analysis, model visualization, and decision tree explanations empower consumers to interpret algorithmic outputs and assess their reliability, accuracy, and relevance in the context of trend marketing strategies.

112

Ethical AI Design Principles:

Transparency in AI algorithms and decision-making processes should be guided by ethical design principles that prioritize fairness, accountability, and interpretability. Businesses should incorporate ethical considerations into the development and deployment of AI technologies, ensuring that algorithms do not perpetuate biases, discrimination, or unintended harm to consumers. Transparent documentation of data sources, model training processes, and evaluation metrics helps mitigate ethical risks and promotes responsible AI use in trend marketing initiatives.

Consumer Control and Consent:

Empowering consumers with control over their data and preferences is essential for promoting transparency in AI-driven marketing strategies. Businesses should provide consumers with transparent options to opt in or opt out of data collection, personalized targeting, and algorithmic decision-making processes. Clear disclosure of data usage policies, consent mechanisms, and privacy settings enables consumers to make informed choices about their participation in AI-powered marketing campaigns and the use of their personal information for trend analysis and targeting purposes.

Auditability and Accountability:

Transparency in AI algorithms and decision-making processes entails establishing mechanisms for auditability and accountability to ensure that algorithmic outcomes align with ethical and legal standards. Businesses should implement processes for auditing AI models, conducting impact assessments, and monitoring algorithmic performance over time. Transparent reporting on algorithmic biases, performance metrics, and decision-making criteria enables stakeholders to assess the reliability, fairness, and accountability of AI-driven marketing strategies and hold businesses accountable for ethical conduct.

Stakeholder Engagement and Education:

Promoting transparency in AI algorithms and decision-making processes requires ongoing engagement and education of stakeholders, including consumers, policymakers, regulators, and industry professionals. Businesses should invest in educational initiatives, public awareness campaigns, and stakeholder forums to raise awareness about AI technologies, demystify algorithmic decision-making, and foster informed discussions about the ethical implications of AI in trend marketing strategies.

Addressing Bias and Fairness in AI-Driven Marketing

In the pursuit of leveraging AI-driven marketing strategies to identify and capitalize on global trends, businesses must prioritize addressing bias and ensuring fairness in algorithmic decision-making processes. Bias in AI algorithms can perpetuate discrimination, reinforce stereotypes, and undermine the credibility and effectiveness of marketing campaigns. In this chapter, we explore the importance of addressing bias and promoting fairness in AI-driven marketing and provide strategies for mitigating bias in the context of trend identification and analysis.

Understanding Bias in AI Algorithms:
Bias in AI algorithms arises from various sources, including biased training data, algorithmic design choices, and inherent human biases embedded in the data. Businesses must recognize the presence of bias in AI systems and understand its implications for marketing strategies. By acknowledging the potential for bias and its impact on decision-making processes, businesses can take proactive steps to identify, mitigate, and prevent biased outcomes in AI-driven marketing initiatives.

Diverse and Representative Data Collection:
Mitigating bias in AI algorithms begins with collecting diverse and representative datasets that accurately reflect the demographics, preferences, and behaviors of target audiences. Businesses should prioritize inclusivity and diversity in data collection efforts, ensuring representation across different demographic groups, geographic regions, and cultural backgrounds. By incorporating diverse perspectives and voices into training datasets, businesses

can mitigate the risk of algorithmic bias and promote fairness in trend analysis and targeting strategies.

Bias Detection and Evaluation Techniques:

Businesses should implement bias detection and evaluation techniques to assess the presence of bias in AI algorithms and decision-making processes. Techniques such as fairness audits, bias impact assessments, and demographic parity analysis enable businesses to identify disparities in algorithmic outcomes across different demographic groups and identify areas for improvement. By quantifying and measuring the impact of bias, businesses can develop targeted strategies to mitigate bias and promote fairness in AI-driven marketing initiatives.

Algorithmic Transparency and Explainability:

Promoting transparency and explainability in AI algorithms is essential for identifying and addressing bias in marketing strategies. Businesses should prioritize the development of transparent and interpretable AI models that provide clear explanations for algorithmic decisions and recommendations. By enabling stakeholders to understand how AI algorithms operate and why specific outcomes are generated, businesses can foster trust, accountability, and scrutiny in the algorithmic decision-making process.

Fairness-Aware Algorithm Design:

Businesses should adopt fairness-aware algorithm design principles to mitigate bias and promote fairness in AI-driven marketing strategies. Fairness-aware algorithms consider fairness constraints and objectives during the model development process, prioritizing equitable outcomes across different demographic groups and mitigating discriminatory effects. Techniques such as fairness constraints, adversarial debiasing, and algorithmic interventions enable businesses to incorporate fairness considerations into AI model training and optimization, reducing the risk of biased outcomes in trend identification and analysis.

Continuous Monitoring and Evaluation:

Addressing bias and

promoting fairness in AI-driven marketing is an ongoing process that requires continuous monitoring, evaluation, and adaptation. Businesses should establish mechanisms for monitoring algorithmic performance, assessing fairness metrics, and soliciting feedback from diverse stakeholders. By regularly evaluating the impact of AI algorithms on different demographic groups and soliciting input from affected communities, businesses can identify emerging biases, address fairness concerns, and refine their marketing strategies to promote inclusivity and equity.

CHAPTER 7

FUTURE TRENDS IN GLOBAL MARKETING AND AI

As the landscape of global marketing continues to evolve, the integration of artificial intelligence (AI) is poised to reshape the way businesses understand consumer behavior, analyze market trends, and execute marketing strategies. Looking ahead, several key trends are expected to shape the future of global marketing in conjunction with AI-driven methodologies. In this chapter, we explore the future trends that are likely to influence the intersection of global marketing and AI.

Hyper-Personalization: The future of global marketing will be characterized by hyper-personalization, where AI algorithms analyze vast amounts of data to deliver personalized experiences tailored to individual preferences, behaviors, and contexts. AI-powered recommendation engines, chatbots, and dynamic content optimization techniques will enable businesses to engage consumers with highly relevant and timely messaging across multiple channels, driving increased engagement, conversion rates, and customer loyalty.

Voice and Visual Search Optimization:

With the rise of voice-enabled devices and visual search technologies, optimizing marketing strategies for voice and visual search will become increasingly important. AI-powered natural language processing (NLP) and computer vision algorithms will enable businesses to understand and respond to voice queries and image-based searches, enhancing discoverability, user experience, and brand visibility in voice-assisted and visual search ecosystems.

Predictive Analytics and Forecasting:

Future marketing strategies will rely heavily on predictive analytics and forecasting techniques to anticipate consumer behavior, identify emerging trends, and adapt marketing campaigns in real-time. AI-driven predictive models will analyze historical data, market trends, and consumer signals to forecast future demand, optimize resource allocation, and drive strategic decision-making across various marketing channels.

Augmented Reality (AR) and Virtual Reality (VR) Experiences:

AR and VR technologies will play a significant role in shaping the future of global marketing by creating immersive brand experiences that captivate audiences and drive engagement. AI algorithms will enhance AR and VR experiences by personalizing content, simulating real-world scenarios, and providing interactive storytelling opportunities that resonate with consumers across diverse demographics and cultural contexts.

Ethical AI and Responsible Marketing Practices:

As AI technologies become more pervasive in global marketing strategies, there will be increased scrutiny and emphasis on ethical AI design principles and responsible marketing practices. Businesses will need to prioritize transparency, fairness, and accountability in AI-driven decision-making processes, address biases and discrimination in algorithmic outputs, and uphold consumer privacy rights to maintain trust and credibility in the eyes of consumers and regulators.

Cross-Channel Integration and Omnichannel Experiences:

The future of global marketing will be characterized by seamless integration and synchronization across multiple marketing channels and touchpoints. AI-powered marketing automation platforms will orchestrate personalized customer journeys, synchronize messaging across channels, and optimize campaign performance in real-time, enabling businesses to deliver cohesive and unified brand experiences that drive engagement and conversion at every stage of the customer lifecycle.

Predictions for the Future of Global Trend Marketing

As we look ahead to the future of global trend marketing, several key predictions emerge that will shape the landscape of marketing strategies, consumer behaviors, and technological advancements. In this chapter, we explore predictions for the future of global trend marketing and the role of AI in driving innovation and transformation.

AI-Powered Predictive Analytics:

Predictive analytics will become increasingly prevalent in global trend marketing, driven by advancements in AI and machine learning algorithms. Businesses will leverage predictive analytics to anticipate consumer preferences, forecast market trends, and optimize marketing strategies in real-time. AI-powered predictive models will analyze vast amounts of data from diverse sources, enabling businesses to make data-driven decisions and stay ahead of emerging trends in the dynamic marketplace.

Emergence of Gen Z as Key Consumer Segment:

Gen Z, the generation born between the mid-1990s and early 2010s, will emerge as a dominant consumer segment shaping global trend marketing strategies. With their digital fluency, social consciousness, and preference for authenticity, Gen Z consumers will demand personalized, purpose-driven marketing experiences that resonate with their values and aspirations. Businesses will need to adapt their marketing strategies to appeal to Gen Z's unique preferences, leverage social media platforms, and engage in cause-driven marketing initiatives to capture this influential consumer segment.

Rise of Influencer Marketing and User-Generated Content:

Influencer marketing and user-generated content will continue to play a significant role in shaping global trend marketing strategies. Businesses will collaborate with influencers, content creators, and brand advocates to amplify their brand message, build authenticity, and foster community engagement. AI-powered sentiment analysis and social listening tools will enable businesses to identify influential voices, track consumer sentiment, and measure the impact of influencer marketing campaigns in real-time.

Expansion of Augmented Reality (AR) and Virtual Reality (VR) Experiences:

Augmented reality (AR) and virtual reality (VR) technologies will revolutionize global trend marketing by creating immersive brand experiences that captivate audiences and drive engagement. Businesses will leverage AR and VR technologies to create interactive product demonstrations, virtual try-on experiences, and immersive storytelling campaigns that blur the lines between physical and digital environments. AI-driven personalization algorithms will enhance AR and VR experiences, delivering tailored content and recommendations based on individual preferences and behaviors.

Ethical AI and Privacy-First Marketing Practices: Ethical AI and privacy-first marketing practices will become increasingly important as consumers become more discerning about data privacy and security. Businesses will prioritize transparency, consent, and data protection in their marketing strategies, adhering to regulatory compliance requirements and consumer expectations for responsible data stewardship. AI-powered privacy-enhancing technologies, such as differential privacy and federated learning, will enable businesses to leverage consumer data for trend analysis and personalization while preserving individual privacy rights and maintaining consumer trust.

Integration of Sustainability and Social Impact Initiatives:

Sustainability and social impact initiatives will be integrated into global trend marketing strategies as consumers demand more socially and environmentally responsible brands. Businesses will align their marketing efforts with sustainable practices, ethical sourcing, and corporate social responsibility (CSR) initiatives to differentiate themselves in the marketplace and appeal to conscious consumer preferences. AI-powered analytics will enable businesses to measure the social and environmental impact of their marketing campaigns, track sustainability metrics, and communicate transparently with consumers about their sustainability efforts.

Innovations in AI Technology and Their Impact on Marketing

Artificial intelligence (AI) technology continues to revolutionize the field of marketing, offering unprecedented capabilities to analyze data, personalize experiences, and optimize campaigns. As AI technologies evolve, their impact on marketing strategies becomes increasingly profound, driving innovation and reshaping the way businesses understand and engage with consumers. In this chapter, we explore key innovations in AI technology and their transformative impact on marketing practices.

Advanced Data Analytics:

Innovations in AI-powered data analytics have revolutionized how businesses interpret and leverage consumer data. Machine learning algorithms can analyze vast datasets in real-time, uncovering hidden patterns, trends, and insights that inform strategic decision-making. Advanced analytics techniques, such as predictive modeling, clustering, and anomaly detection, enable marketers to anticipate consumer behavior, identify market trends, and optimize campaign performance with unprecedented accuracy and efficiency.

Natural Language Processing (NLP): Natural language processing (NLP) technology enables AI systems to understand, interpret, and generate human language, opening up new possibilities for conversational marketing and customer engagement. Chatbots, virtual assistants, and voice-enabled interfaces powered by NLP algorithms can deliver personalized customer support, facilitate sales interactions, and provide relevant recommendations based on natural language queries and conversational context, enhancing the overall customer experience.

Computer Vision: Computer vision technology allows AI systems to interpret and analyze visual content, including images, videos, and graphics. By leveraging computer vision algorithms, marketers can extract valuable insights from visual data, such as consumer preferences, product attributes, and brand sentiment. Visual search capabilities enable consumers to discover products based on images, while augmented reality (AR) and virtual reality (VR) experiences offer immersive brand interactions that drive engagement and brand loyalty.

Personalization at Scale: AI-driven personalization algorithms empower marketers to deliver highly personalized experiences at scale across multiple channels and touchpoints. By analyzing consumer behavior, preferences, and demographics, AI systems can tailor content, product recommendations, and messaging to individual users in real-time, increasing relevance and resonance. Personalization enhances customer engagement, fosters brand loyalty, and drives conversion rates by delivering customized experiences that align with consumer preferences and interests.

Marketing Automation and Optimization: AI-powered marketing automation platforms streamline campaign management processes, automate repetitive tasks, and optimize marketing performance across the entire customer journey. From lead generation and nurturing to conversion and retention, AI algorithms orchestrate personalized customer interactions, segment audiences dynamically, and deliver targeted messaging at the right time and on the right channel. Marketing automation drives operational efficiency, accelerates time-to-market, and maximizes ROI by optimizing resource allocation and campaign effectiveness.

Predictive Modeling and Forecasting:

Predictive modeling techniques leverage historical data and machine learning algorithms to forecast future trends, identify potential opportunities, and mitigate risks in marketing strategies. By analyzing past performance metrics, market dynamics, and consumer behavior patterns, predictive models can anticipate customer churn, predict demand fluctuations, and optimize advertising spend allocation. Predictive analytics empowers marketers to make data-driven decisions, adapt strategies proactively, and capitalize on emerging trends in the dynamic marketplace.

Strategies for Staying Ahead of Future Trends

In the dynamic landscape of global trend marketing, staying ahead of future trends is essential for businesses to maintain relevance, capitalize on emerging opportunities, and sustain competitive advantage. As the intersection of AI and marketing continues to evolve, businesses must adopt proactive strategies to anticipate, analyze, and adapt to evolving trends effectively. In this chapter, we explore key strategies for staying ahead of future trends in global trend marketing.

Continuous Monitoring and Analysis: Implement a robust system for continuous monitoring and analysis of market trends, consumer behavior, and industry developments. Leverage AI-powered analytics tools to collect and process real-time data from diverse sources, including social media platforms, market research reports, and industry publications. Stay informed about emerging trends, shifting consumer preferences, and competitor strategies to identify new opportunities and adapt marketing strategies accordingly.

Investment in AI Technologies: Embrace AI technologies and invest in cutting-edge AI solutions to enhance

marketing capabilities and drive innovation. Explore AI-driven predictive analytics, natural language processing, and machine learning algorithms to uncover actionable insights, predict future trends, and optimize campaign performance. Collaborate with AI experts, data scientists, and technology partners to leverage AI technologies effectively and gain a competitive edge in the marketplace.

Customer-Centric Approach:

Prioritize a customer-centric approach to marketing by understanding and addressing the evolving needs, preferences, and expectations of target audiences. Conduct market research, customer surveys, and sentiment analysis to gain insights into consumer behavior and sentiment. Personalize marketing campaigns, product offerings, and customer experiences to create meaningful connections with consumers and foster brand loyalty in an increasingly competitive landscape.

Agile Decision-Making Processes: Cultivate a culture of agility

and adaptability within the organization to respond quickly to changing market dynamics and consumer trends. Empower cross-functional teams to make data-driven decisions, experiment with new ideas, and iterate on marketing strategies in real-time. Embrace agile methodologies, rapid prototyping, and test-and-learn approaches to optimize campaign performance and capitalize on emerging opportunities.

Strategic Partnerships and Collaborations: Foster strategic partnerships and collaborations with industry stakeholders, technology providers, and thought leaders to stay abreast of industry trends and innovations. Participate in industry events, conferences, and networking forums to exchange ideas, share best practices, and explore potential collaborations. Collaborate with academic institutions, research organizations, and innovation hubs to access cutting-edge research, insights, and technologies that drive future trends in global marketing.

Investment in Talent and Training: Invest in talent development and training initiatives to equip employees with the skills, knowledge, and competencies needed to navigate the evolving landscape of global trend marketing. Provide opportunities for continuous learning, professional development, and upskilling in areas such as AI, data analytics, and digital marketing. Foster a culture of innovation, creativity, and knowledge sharing to inspire employees to embrace change, explore new ideas, and drive future trends in marketing.

Ethical and Responsible Practices: Prioritize ethical and responsible marketing practices that prioritize consumer trust, data privacy, and transparency. Adhere to industry standards, regulatory requirements, and ethical guidelines governing data usage, advertising practices, and consumer engagement. Communicate transparently with consumers about data collection practices, privacy policies, and the use of AI technologies in marketing campaigns to build trust and credibility in the marketplace.

CHAPTER 8

CONCLUSION

In the rapidly evolving landscape of global trend marketing, the integration of artificial intelligence (AI) has emerged as a transformative force, enabling businesses to navigate complexities, anticipate shifts, and capitalize on emerging opportunities with unprecedented precision and agility. Throughout this book, we have explored the convergence of AI and marketing, delving into strategies, technologies, and best practices for leveraging AI in the pursuit of global trend marketing objectives.

From the foundational principles of understanding consumer behavior to the application of advanced AI technologies in trend analysis and predictive modeling, businesses have gained valuable insights into harnessing the power of AI to drive strategic outcomes and achieve sustainable growth. We have examined the significance of transparency, ethics, and responsible practices in AI-driven marketing, emphasizing the importance of building consumer trust, protecting data privacy, and upholding ethical standards in the pursuit of marketing excellence.

As we conclude our journey into the realm of global trend marketing strategy, it is evident that the future holds immense promise and potential for businesses that embrace innovation, adaptability, and consumer-centricity. The convergence of AI technologies, big data analytics, and digital platforms will continue to reshape the dynamics of marketing, offering new opportunities for engagement, personalization, and brand-building in an increasingly interconnected world.

However, with opportunity comes responsibility. As businesses harness the power of AI to unlock insights, personalize experiences, and optimize campaigns, it is imperative to prioritize ethical considerations, transparency, and consumer welfare. By upholding ethical principles, respecting consumer privacy, and fostering trust and transparency, businesses can build enduring relationships with consumers and contribute to a more sustainable and equitable marketing ecosystem.

As we look towards the future, it is clear that the journey of global trend marketing strategy powered by AI is one of continuous evolution and adaptation. By embracing change, fostering innovation, and staying attuned to emerging trends, businesses can position themselves as leaders in the dynamic and ever-evolving landscape of global trend marketing.

We hope that this book has served as a valuable resource for marketers, business leaders, and professionals seeking to navigate the complexities of global trend marketing strategy in the age of AI. May the insights, strategies, and best practices shared within these pages inspire you to embark on a journey of discovery, innovation, and success in your pursuit of global trend marketing excellence.

Recap of Key Points

"Understanding Global Trend Marketing Strategy: Using AI in Finding the Current Marketing Trend" explores the intersection of artificial intelligence (AI) and marketing strategies to navigate the complexities of global trend marketing. Throughout the book, several key points have been emphasized to help businesses leverage AI effectively in their marketing endeavors:

Foundations of Global Trend Marketing:

The book underscores the importance of understanding consumer behavior, market dynamics, and emerging trends as foundational elements of global trend marketing. By analyzing consumer insights and market data, businesses can identify opportunities, anticipate shifts, and capitalize on emerging trends with precision and agility.

Role of AI in Marketing Trends:

AI technologies play a pivotal role in analyzing vast amounts of data, uncovering insights, and driving informed decision-making in marketing strategies. From predictive analytics to personalized recommendations, AI empowers businesses to enhance targeting, optimize campaigns, and deliver personalized experiences that resonate with consumers.

Ethical Considerations in AI-driven Marketing:

Ethical considerations, transparency, and consumer privacy are paramount in AI-driven marketing strategies. Businesses must prioritize ethical practices, respect consumer privacy rights, and foster transparency in data collection, algorithmic decision-making, and personalized targeting to build trust and credibility with consumers.

Innovations in AI Technology:

The book explores cutting-edge innovations in AI technology, including natural language processing, computer vision, and predictive modeling, and their transformative impact on marketing practices. By embracing AI-driven solutions, businesses can unlock new insights, optimize campaign performance, and drive meaningful engagement with consumers across diverse channels and touchpoints.

Strategies for Staying Ahead of Trends:

Proactive strategies such as continuous monitoring, investment in AI technologies, customer-centricity, agile decision-making, strategic partnerships, talent development, and ethical practices are essential for staying ahead of future trends in global trend marketing. By embracing innovation, adapting to change, and prioritizing consumer needs, businesses can position themselves as leaders in the dynamic landscape of global trend marketing.

Conclusion and Future Outlook:

As the book concludes, it emphasizes the promising future of global trend marketing powered by AI technologies. By fostering innovation, upholding ethical principles, and staying attuned to emerging trends, businesses can drive sustainable growth, build enduring relationships with consumers, and thrive in the evolving landscape of global trend marketing.

Overall, "Understanding Global Trend Marketing Strategy: Using AI in Finding the Current Marketing Trend" provides invaluable insights, strategies, and best practices for businesses seeking to harness the power of AI in navigating the complexities of global trend marketing and driving success in an increasingly interconnected world.

Final Thoughts on the Intersection of AI and Global Trend Marketing

As we conclude our exploration of the intersection of AI and global trend marketing, it is evident that the convergence of these two domains represents a paradigm shift in how businesses understand, engage with, and influence consumer behavior in the digital age. The marriage of AI technologies with marketing strategies has unlocked unprecedented opportunities for businesses to navigate the complexities of the global marketplace, anticipate shifts in consumer preferences, and capitalize on emerging trends with agility and precision.

At the heart of this intersection lies the transformative power of data. AI technologies enable businesses to harness the vast troves of data generated by consumers, social media platforms, and digital interactions to uncover insights, identify patterns, and derive actionable intelligence that informs strategic decision-making. From predictive analytics to personalized recommendations, AI-driven insights empower marketers to optimize campaigns, enhance targeting, and deliver personalized experiences that resonate with consumers across diverse channels and touchpoints.

However, with great power comes great responsibility. As businesses embrace AI technologies to drive marketing strategies, it is imperative to prioritize ethical considerations, transparency, and consumer privacy. Upholding ethical principles, respecting consumer rights, and fostering transparency in data collection and algorithmic decision-making are essential for building trust and credibility with consumers in an increasingly data-driven world.

Furthermore, the journey of AI and global trend marketing is one of continuous evolution and adaptation. The landscape is dynamic, trends are fleeting, and consumer preferences are ever-changing. To stay ahead of the curve, businesses must embrace innovation, agility, and a customer-centric mindset. Continuous monitoring, investment in AI technologies, strategic partnerships, and talent development are essential strategies for navigating the shifting currents of global trend marketing and driving sustainable growth in an increasingly competitive marketplace.

As we look towards the future, the possibilities are limitless. The intersection of AI and global trend marketing holds the promise of unlocking new insights, creating personalized experiences, and driving meaningful engagement with consumers in ways that were once unimaginable. By embracing innovation, upholding ethical standards, and staying attuned to emerging trends, businesses can chart a course towards success in the dynamic and ever-evolving landscape of global trend marketing powered by AI technologies.

In closing, let us embrace the opportunities, navigate the challenges, and embark on a journey of discovery, innovation, and growth at the intersection of AI and global trend marketing. Together, we can harness the power of technology to create meaningful connections, drive positive change, and shape the future of marketing in the digital era.

Call to Action: Embrace AI for Trend Analysis and Strategy

Dear Marketers,

As we navigate the dynamic landscape of global trend marketing, one thing is abundantly clear: the future belongs to those who embrace innovation, adapt to change, and harness the power of technology to drive success. In our quest to stay ahead of the curve and capitalize on emerging trends, there is one tool that stands out as a game-changer: artificial intelligence (AI).

AI has revolutionized the way we understand consumer behavior, analyze market trends, and execute marketing strategies. With its unparalleled ability to process vast amounts of data, uncover hidden insights, and predict future trends, AI has become an indispensable ally in the pursuit of marketing excellence.

Today, we stand at the cusp of a new era in global trend marketing—one where AI-driven insights fuel strategic decision-making, personalized experiences captivate audiences, and data-driven approaches redefine the boundaries of what's possible. It's time for us to seize this opportunity and embrace AI for trend analysis and strategy like never before.

Here's our call to action:

Embrace Innovation: Embrace AI as a catalyst for innovation in your marketing strategies. Explore AI-powered tools and technologies that enable you to analyze data, predict trends, and optimize campaigns with precision and efficiency.

Harness Data Insights: Leverage AI to unlock actionable insights from your data. Dive deep into consumer behavior patterns, market trends, and competitive dynamics to uncover hidden opportunities and drive strategic decision-making.

Personalize Experiences: Embrace AI-driven personalization to deliver tailored experiences that resonate with your audience. Leverage predictive analytics and recommendation engines to deliver the right message, to the right person, at the right time.

Stay Agile and Adaptive: Adopt an agile and adaptive mindset to navigate the rapidly evolving landscape of global trend marketing. Embrace experimentation, iterate on your strategies, and pivot quickly in response to changing market dynamics.

Prioritize Ethical Practices: Uphold ethical standards and prioritize consumer privacy in all your AI-driven marketing endeavors. Respect consumer rights, foster transparency, and build trust with your audience through responsible data stewardship.

By embracing AI for trend analysis and strategy, we have the opportunity to unlock new possibilities, drive meaningful engagement, and shape the future of marketing in the digital era. Let's come together, embrace innovation, and harness the power of AI to propel our businesses forward in the dynamic and ever-evolving landscape of global trend marketing.